Thinking Strategically Within Nonprofits

Every Organization Is Created for a Purpose; Thinking Strategically Will Achieve That Purpose

Michael S. Doré
in collaboration with
Barry Silverberg

Austin, Texas

Thinking Strategically Within Nonprofits
Every Organization Is Created for a Purpose; Thinking Strategically Will Achieve That Purpose

Michael S Doré

© Michael S Doré, 2003
1st World Library
8015 Shoal Creek Blvd., Ste. 100
Austin, TX 78757
www.1stworldlibrary.com

Second Edition

Managing Editor
Barry Silverberg

Cover Design and Production
Amelia Nottingham-Martin

Library of Congress Card Catalog Number: 2003100711

ISBN: 0-9718562-5-7

All rights reserved. No part of this book may be reproduced, utilized in any form or by any means, electronic, or mechanical, including photocopying or recording, or by any information storage and retrieval system, without permission in writing from the author.

Dedication

To my loving wife, Ruth, who has always believed I have books in me.

Acknowledgements

The man who taught me about strategic planning is C. Davis (Dave) Fogg. When I left IBM and was looking for a job, he hired me to be a consultant for his firm out of Nashville. The first thing he did was to train me how to teach the three-day course in Strategic Planning for the American Management Association. Then he brought me on board to be part of various consulting engagements with his firm.

A guiding force during the four years we spent together was his first book, *Team Based Strategic Planning*. Later, as I taught classes in various universities, that book became the text I used in my classes. From the ideas he shared in that book and from my experience working with him, I have been able to capture the minds of many executives and leaders as they developed plans for their futures.

Dave, thank you for teaching me what has become the center of my consulting life.

Preface

Thinking strategically within nonprofits is no longer a luxury. It is a necessity.

In collaborating on this book, I helped translate Michael Doré's 35 years of global business experience into a body of work immediately applicable to the nonprofit arena. Indeed, most of the strategic thinking and planning in "business" become self-evident approaches and tools for nonprofits once we speak of "stakeholders" in addition to the more widely used "customer" in business literature.

The major difference between nonprofits and for-profits lies in ownership and accountability. In for-profits, ownership rests with the partners or stockholders. They make the investments, take the financial risks, and enjoy the positive or negative consequences of their own decisions. Management is accountable to them and they are largely accountable to themselves.

The public owns nonprofits. Members of nonprofit Boards are accountable to the public through the office of their state attorney general. The public provides nonprofits with special privileges such as tax exemption and the nonprofit provides services that enhance the public welfare.

While for-profits have stockholders, nonprofits have stakeholders.

Borrowing from the phenomenal work of Burt Namus, *Visionary Leadership, Creating A Compelling Sense of Direction*

For Your Organization (Jossey-Bass Publishers, San Francisco, 1992), we employ his definition of "stakeholder" in this book:

"A stakeholder is anyone who has the power to exert an influence on your organization or who is strongly influenced by your organization in some significant way. A stakeholder may be a single person, a group of individuals, or another large organization or institution. Each has a unique involvement with your organization and differing interests, priorities, and expectations."

Analyzing the state of a nonprofit, visioning its future, and taking the steps to implement that future is what this first volume of a planned series on *Thinking Strategically Within Nonprofits* is all about.

We hope you will find this work a pragmatic tool to help you position your nonprofit agency where you and your stakeholders wish it to be.

Barry Silverberg

Austin, Texas

January 2003

Table of Contents

Preface   i
Introduction   1
   Why is a plan needed?   4

Chapter One
Putting the Plan Into Context   9
   Question Two: "What do we do?" — Process   10
   Question Three: "For whom do we do it?" — Consumers   11
   Question Four: "What do they want?" - Quality   12
   Question Five: "How do we deliver it?"— Process Management   13
   Question Six: "How are we doing?" — Measurement   15
   Question Seven: "Do others do it better?" — Benchmarking   17
   Question Eight: "How do we do better?" — Process Improvement   19
   Question Nine: "How will we work?" — Teamwork   21
   Question Ten: "How will we tell about our services?" — Marketing   22
   Question Eleven: "How will we lead our organization?"— Leadership   27
   Question Twelve: "Will our consumers be delighted? — Consumer Satisfaction   29

Chapter Two
Overview of the Strategic Planning Process   31

   Question One: Where are we going? - Plan   31
   The Strategic Planning Process   32
   Achieving Results   37

Chapter Three
Gathering Information Prior to Priority Setting   41

Chapter Four
Environmental Assumptions   45

   Potential Environmental Factors   45
   Planning Assumptions   56

Chapter Five
Market and Competitive Analysis   59

   Segment Analysis   59
   Consumer Wants and Needs   64
   Importance vs. Performance   68
   Competitive Analysis   70
   Competitive Advantage   73
   Products and Services   77
   Financial Analysis   82

Chapter Six
SWOTs and Priority Issues — 85

Table 10 is Strengths, Weaknesses, Opportunities, and Threats (SWOT).	85
Table 11 is Strategic Priority Issues (PIs).	89
Table 12 is Focal Areas for Priority Issues.	91
Consensus on SWOTs and Priority Issues	94

Chapter Seven
Objective and Strategy Setting — 97

Mission Statement Review	97
Focal Areas and Measures	98
Objectives	99
Strategic Alternatives	100
Final Strategies and Strategy Teams	102
Action Plans	103
Review	112
Plan Wrap Up	122
Conclusion	125

Glossary — 127

Appendix — 131

Index — 139

Table of Charts

Figure 1: Twelve Questions for Achieving Your Organization's Purpose	3
Figure 2: The Basic Planning Cycle	6
Figure 3: Balanced Scorecard	16
Figure 4: Marketing	23
Figure 5: Overview of the Strategic Planning Process	33
Figure 6: Potential Environmental Factors	46-48
Worksheet 1: The Organization's External Factors	49
HelpingUHelp Worksheet 1: The Organization's External Factors	49
Figure 7: Analyzing the External Environment	51
Table 1: External Trends Summary	52
HelpingUHelp Table 1: External Trends Summary	53
Table 2: Opportunities and Threats	54
HelpingUHelp Table 2: Opportunities and Threats	55
Table 3: Key Planning Assumptions	57
HelpingUHelp Table 3: Key Planning Assumptions	57
Table 4: Key Market Segments	62
HelpingUHelp Table 4: Key Market Segments	63
Worksheet 2: Consumer Wants and Needs	64
HelpingUHelp Worksheet 2: Consumer Wants and Needs	65
Table 5: Key Consumer Wants and Needs	66
HelpingUHelp Table 5: Key Consumer Wants and Needs	67
Figure 8: Performance Matrix	68
Figure 9: Completed Performance Matrix	69
Table 6: Key Competitors	71
HelpingUHelp Table 6: Key Competitors	72

Table 7: Competitive Advantage	75
HelpingUHelp Table 7: Competitive Advantage	76
Table 8a: Products and Services (A-C)	78
HelpingUHelp Table 8a: Products and Services (A-C)	79
Table 8b: Products and Services (D-H)	80
HelpingUHelp Table 8b: Products and Services (D-H)	81
Table 9: Finances	83
HelpingUHelp Table 9: Finances	84
Figure 10: Analyzing the Internal Environment	86
Table 10: Organization's Strengths, Weaknesses, Opportunities, and Threats (SWOTS)	88
HelpingUHelp Table 10: Organization's Strengths, Weaknesses, Opportunities, and Threats (SWOTS)	89
Table 11: Strategic Priority Issues	90
HelpingUHelp Table 11: Strategic Priority Issues	90
Table 12: Focal Areas for Priority Issues	92
HelpingUHelp Table 12: Focal Areas for Priority Issues	93
Table 13: Strategic Alternatives	101
HelpingUHelp Table 13: Strategic Alternatives	102
Action Plan Form A	106
HelpingUHelp Action Plan Form A	108
Action Plan Form A1	110
HelpingUHelp Action Plan Form A1	111
Review - Form B	113
Quarterly Review- Form C	114-116
HelpingUHelp Quarterly Review- From C	118-120
Outline of a Strategic Plan - Form D	124

Introduction

Every organization is created for a purpose. To achieve that purpose, its professional and volunteer leaders and all wishing it success, need to think strategically.

Thinking strategically, at its most elemental, is a process of clarifying the organization's purpose, positing its desired future, and systematically addressing the challenges and opportunities before the organization.

In the following pages, we will explore together what it takes to achieve an organization's purpose. While the principles and processes are drawn from the best practices and thinking of the for-profit world, they have been applied to the nonprofit arena many, many times and have proven successful.

So without further ado, let's explore what it takes to achieve an organization's purpose.

An organizational purpose has two focal points:

1. The **consumer** (known as the customer in for-profit organizations) or entity who receives the output or product of the organization (e.g., the stakeholders, client, donor, etc.); and

2. The **results** or payback to the organization itself from providing what its consumers needs (e.g., program services, dollars, products, etc.)

A good organization will focus first and foremost on the consumer, knowing that by satisfying the consumer it will bring about results that will make the organization thrive in the future.

Focusing on how to satisfy the consumer is basically a series of logical steps that start with describing what the organization is doing for the consumer.

To do this, the organization must ask:

- Whether those things are what the consumer wants,
- How well they are being done, and
- If they can be improved.

A critical aspect of managing a nonprofit organization is ensuring that consumers or stakeholders are satisfied with the processes the organization uses to serve them.

To achieve this, the organization's leaders must pay attention to all the factors impacting its strategic and financial results or payback. In the process of developing the long-range strategic plan, the organization has the most likely opportunity to achieve both full consumer satisfaction and attractive organizational results – i.e., achieve its purpose.

There are twelve basic questions a nonprofit (or any) organization should ask as it seeks success. They address the many aspects of leading and managing an organization. Starting from the broadest, these questions progressively focus a nonprofit organization's leaders on the fundamental challenges and opportunities that require their primary attention. These questions are left unaddressed at the leaders' and organization's peril!

Figure 1
Twelve Questions for Achieving Your Organization's Purpose

1.	Where are we going?	*Plan*
2.	What do we do?	*Process*
3.	For whom do we do it?	*Consumer*
4.	What do they want?	*Quality*
5.	How do we deliver it?	*Process management*
6.	How are we doing?	*Measurement*
7.	Do others do it better?	*Benchmarking*
8.	How can we do better?	*Process improvement*
9.	How will we work?	*Teamwork*
10.	How will we tell about our service?	*Marketing*
11.	How will we lead our organization?	*Leadership*
12.	Will our consumer be delighted?	*Consumer Satisfaction*

Why is a plan needed?

A plan helps chart the process and the resources needed by the organization to achieve its purpose. As important as the resulting document may be, it is the very process of developing the plan that provides the greatest benefits. No less a master planner than Dwight D. Eisenhower, the planner of D-Day and the liberation of Europe in World War II, said: "Plans are useless; planning is everything!"

What Eisenhower encapsulated in that statement is the importance of engaging the right people and gathering the right information to create a plan that does more than fill space on a shelf. And there are more strategic plans filling shelves in organizations than we may ever wish to count.

Our focus is on developing a plan that satisfies your organization's consumers and helps you achieve your organizational purpose. Accordingly, planning should be understood as a process: a series of steps to be accomplished as a team.

No organization can operate successfully without a team-based overall plan that can be broken down into functional or departmental work plans for its people to follow. Depending on your organization's size and operational complexity, a team of five to twelve functional leaders will provide the coordination that makes the planning process work, from development through deployment.

Imagine a military campaign without a strategy or plan. Imagine the leader not knowing his troops' strengths and weaknesses or not knowing what his opportunities and threats are in various battle situations. Imagine the leader not knowing of the strengths and weaknesses or the whereabouts of his enemy. Imagine his troops not having specific tactics to employ in concert with each other during the battle. These imaginings are no different from a campaign to do the daily job of any organization.

Some organizations operate with the "Fire, ready, aim" mentality decried in Tom Peter's and Bob Waterman's *In Search of Excellence*. The "Just do it" catch phrase of one American firm is another expression of this philosophy; though this latter company has a strategic plan that reflects anything but a "just do it" approach.

It is a serious mistake for any organization, and especially a nonprofit with limited time and resources, to not take the time to plan before acting. Without due diligence, of which strategic planning is a major part, an organization quickly finds itself facing challenges that it might have otherwise anticipated and facing opportunities for which it is not adequately prepared to take advantage.

Thinking through how to achieve the organization's purpose, or a specific problem to solve, it is far wiser (and ultimately less expensive in terms of time, energy and other resources) to stop and **think, agree, act,** and **evaluate**; in other words to develop a plan, deploy it, and see if it works.

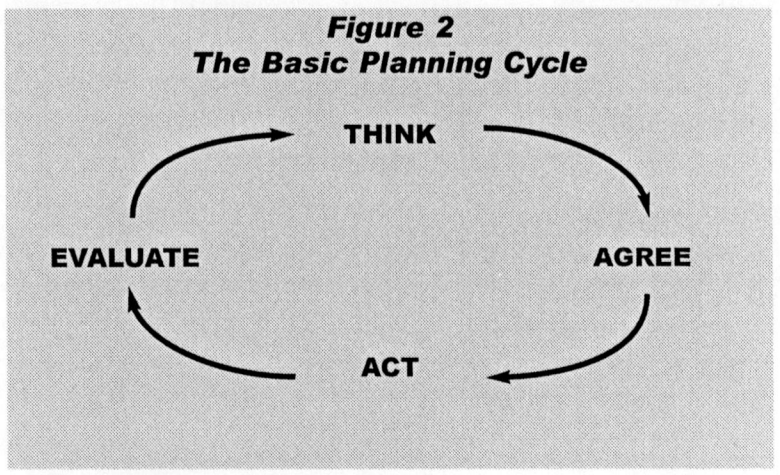

The Basic Planning Cycle

The basic planning process begins with those selected to lead the process:

1. *THINKING* **carefully and deciding how they will go about solving the problem or developing the plan.**

    Determining what methodology or approach they will use as a process for accomplishing their purpose

    Deciding the roles they will play in this process and how much time they will devote to it.

2. *AGREEING* **on all the factors or elements used in the process.**

    Identifying the elements and then qualifying or quantifying them. This is where the team determines things like strengths, weaknesses, opportunities, and threats. It is where they agree on mission and objectives; and where strategies and the actions to implement them are developed.

3. *ACTING* **or implementing the strategic alternatives the team has chosen as part of their "agreeing" process.**

    Avoiding the strong tendency to do something as quickly as possible. Many employees think their superiors will be impressed when they act or make something happen quickly in a situation. Who has time for thinking and agreeing in this busy, competitive world? Someone else may beat us to the punch.

4. *EVALUATING* **whether the actions worked.**

    Did it achieve the objectives they had agreed upon? If it didn't, they should return to the agree process and choose another alternative and act upon it. Either the first or another of their alternatives will work and they will see the good results of this four-step process.

Chapter One

Putting the Plan Into Context

While the majority of this book deals with the first of our twelve questions in Figure 1, it is important for us to understand what lies behind all twelve questions even before we confront the challenges of answering the fundamental question of "Where are we going?"

To answer the first question of "where are we going?" we mainly use our brains. Primarily we need to think through the question to understand all aspects of our organization's plan. The other eleven questions require far more hands and feet, in addition to our brain. They require exploration of the resources and tools to be used in our plan.

By understanding what is entailed in answering these other questions, team members will be more effective in thinking strategically and in integrating the various components into a coherent overall plan.

So let's briefly explore questions 2 through 12 before returning to our in-depth treatment of all that is entailed in developing a plan to answer the most fundamental of all questions a nonprofit organization faces: "Where are we going?"

Our intention is to go into greater depth on these questions in future volumes.

Question Two: "What do we do?" — Process

Processes are the vehicles through which real work gets done in any organization. They are, in essence, what organizations do to achieve their purpose.

The only way to achieve the plan your organization will develop is through processes. They are the activities involving people, equipment, energy, procedures, and material that take measurable inputs, add value to them, and produce measurable outputs to internal or external consumers.

A process is what a person does in his or her job. For optimal organizational success, all employees of an organization should know the processes for which they are responsible in accomplishing consumer requirements and business goals. With this understanding, employees see how their efforts relate to other processes in their or other functions. When everyone in the organization sees the interrelationships and interdependence of one process on another, they can work together productively and truly accomplish the organization's strategic plan.

Question Three: "For whom do we do it?" — Consumers

Consumers are why a nonprofit organization exists. The plan, and most of the processes, will be focused on satisfying the interests and needs of the organization's consumers (e.g., the stakeholders, clients, donors, etc.). Simply put, consumer satisfaction is the driving force behind any nonprofit organization.

If the nonprofit organization does not fully appreciate who the consumers are and what their wants and needs are, all the organization's efforts are wasted. As such, the key to the twelve questions for success is to always focus first and foremost on consumers and what they want and need. Every other question relates directly to meeting consumer expectations.

The steps to creating a consumer-driven nonprofit organization can be summarized in seven imperatives[1]:

1. Create a consumer-keeping vision
2. Saturate your organization with the voice of the consumer
3. Go to school on the winners
4. Liberate your consumer champions
5. Smash the barriers to consumer-winning performance
6. Measure, measure, measure
7. Walk the talk

[1] *The Customer Driven Company: Moving From Talk to Action.* Whiteley, Richard C., Addison Wesley, 1991

These imperatives relate to a number of the other questions. When acting on those questions, always think back to the consumer and how they impact of affect him or her.

Question Four: "What do they want?" – Quality

What consumers want from the nonprofit organization is <u>quality</u>.

Quality may be something only the consumer can describe. It may be a particular set of features in a product or service. It may be something that satisfies a particular user's needs. It may be something that meets a design specification. It may be a product or service of a certain value. In simple terms, the people in any nonprofit organization should realize that consumers define quality as having their particular requirements met. A basic definition of quality is "meeting a consumer's requirements."

If the organization has not determined the consumer's definition of quality, it cannot hope to meet the consumer's or their own business objectives.

Quality is a critical aspect of every nonprofit organization and its success. While quality ends up being visible to the consumer in the final product or service, it starts in every employee and the way they perform their jobs. Therefore, it is integral to every process.

Quality and process are two sides of the same coin. You cannot have one without the other. Quality is not something to be inspected into products and services after they are produced. In the processes they use to develop those products and services, employees must ensure they conform to consumer requirements and deliver total quality in everything they do.

Question Five: "How do we deliver it?"— Process Management

To deliver the quality expected and satisfy the needs of consumers, the organization must ensure all of its processes work the way they should.

Process Management defines all the nonprofit organization's processes and documents and maps them. It identifies consumer and stakeholder requirements and sets standards for measuring their performance, benchmarking them, and performing root cause analysis.

Process management relates to the assessment and analysis of an organization's processes. It involves identifying its core and key processes and introduces a set of steps to manage them effectively and efficiently to meet organizational objectives.

From their processes, employees should expect:

- **Effectiveness** Producing desired results for the consumer: The right output at the right place, at the right time, at the right cost
- **Efficiency** Minimizing the resources used: An output in the shortest time at the least cost

- **Adaptability**   Adapting to changing consumer and business needs:
  Meeting today's special needs and future requirements

Process management applies the nonprofit organization's plan and ensures that everything people do in their jobs supports that plan. The process management process involves:

- Identifying all processes and the individual or team that owns them
- Determining consumer requirements for the process
- Documenting how the process is performed
- Mapping the process
- Rating or evaluating the process
- Benchmarking the process against better processes
- Determining root causes of problems in the process

Organizational benefits from properly managing processes include:

- Consumer satisfaction resulting from good performance in quality and excellence in all key areas related to meeting consumer needs
- Low cost from lack of rework or redundancy in processes
- Clearly-defined and agreed-upon requirements and performance targets
- Consensus across functions on direction, vision, and priorities
- Good communications among all functions and levels of management

Question Six: "How are we doing?" — Measurement

Every nonprofit organization should decide its four or five most important questions for success and measure the answers it finds as it operates. Every question and area we identify here must be measured.

To manage processes it is important to measure the inputs, the value added, and the outputs for each process. Consumer satisfaction with the organization's products and services and processes must be measured. The quality of every employee, their work, and their accomplishments must be measured.

The specific objectives for each strategy within the plan must be measured periodically to determine if the plan is being met.

If something is not measured, it is not important. But measurement can be overdone.

Every nonprofit organization should decide the four or five most important areas it is focusing on and measure how well it is performing in each of those areas. To avoid overdoing measurement, it is useful to apply the philosophy of a "Balanced Scorecard":

1. To bring focus and consistency to measurement, start by defining every thing that should be measured across all activities—in the plan, in processes, with consumers, in finances, and in quality, to name a few. In the planning process to be discussed below, the Objectives section defines the many areas to be measured.

2. With the list of measurements defined, next decide the few most important high-level drivers of the organization and its business situation. These might be things like the consumer, internal operations, people, innovation, and finances.
3. Review the long list of many measurements across all activities and group them under one of the high level drivers.
4. Track each sub-measurement but report them to senior management from the perspective of the critical high-level driver.

A typical Balanced Scorecard is shown below. All the key areas your organization is measuring will revolve around your vision:

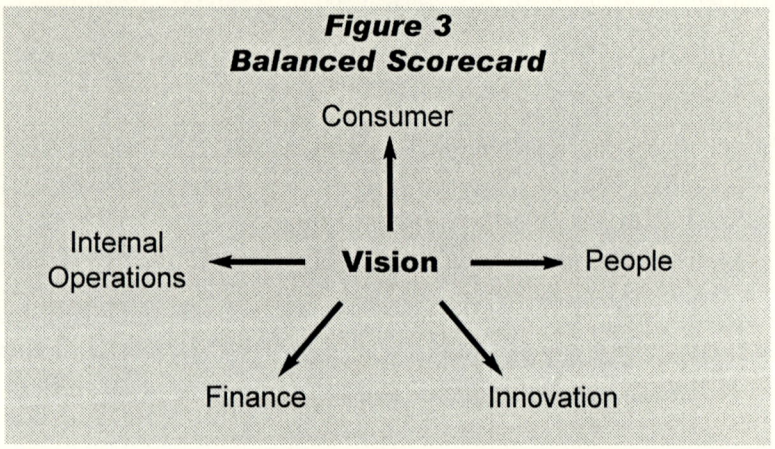

**Figure 3
Balanced Scorecard**

You will have a number of measurements under Consumer, under Internal Operations, under People, under Innovation, and under Finance. This five-item balanced scorecard will allow managers and employees to look at the business from these five most important perspectives. In the above example, it provides the answer to five basic questions of success[2]:

- Are our consumers satisfied?
- What must we excel at in our operations?
- Are our people happy and productive?
- Are we innovating in creating value?
- How are we doing financially?

As noted above, every nonprofit organization should decide its four or five most important questions and measure the answers it finds as it operates.

Question Seven: "Do others do it better?" — Benchmarking

The very best organizations use benchmarking widely in every process or function. It is a never-ending discovery and learning experience that identifies and evaluates best processes and performance in order to integrate them into the organization to increase effectiveness, efficiency, and adaptability. It is a critical part of the success of an organization. "Firms that have realized the value of focusing on business processes recognize there can be a

---

[2] "The Balanced Scorecard - Measures That Drive Performance", Kaplan, Robert S. and Norton, David P., *Harvard Business Review*, January-February 1992

high-level awareness of the need for change by driving the key performance measures established through benchmarking."[3]

Benchmarking provides a systematic way to discover superior processes, products, services, and practices that can be adopted or adapted to the nonprofit organization's environment to reduce costs, decrease cycle time, cut inventory, and provide greater satisfaction to internal and external consumers.

Benchmarking is like a detective story. It searches through the many clues available in the public domain to find leads which identify the truly world-class processes or approaches other organizations use to run their operation. Unless they are copyrighted or patented, it is alright to use these new ideas in your organization. And those ideas can come from other nonprofit organizations as well as from the for-profit sector or government. Xerox went to L.L. Bean to benchmark their distribution processes. Then they won the Malcom Baldrige Award.

Benchmarking is as useful in goal-setting as it is in process management. By looking at organizations that are more successful, your team can determine and set challenging targets and goals. Since someone else already met these targets, your organization knows they are attainable. Setting such goals can improve performance and provide a competitive advantage.

---

[3] *Business Process Benchmarking: Finding and Implementing Best Practices*, Camp, Robert C. ASQC Quality Press, 1995

Benchmarking is a ten-step process[4]:

1. Decide what will be benchmarked
2. Identify whom to benchmark
3. Plan and conduct the benchmark investigation
4. Determine the current performance gap between your and their results
5. Project future performance levels from using new ideas
6. Communicate benchmark findings and gain acceptance
7. Establish new performance goals
8. Develop action plans
9. Implement plans and monitor progress
10. Recalibrate benchmarks to stay current

Question Eight: "How do we do better?" — Process Improvement

Continuous improvement of processes is a basic practice of all the world's good organizations – nonprofit or for-profit. Every organization needs some form of continuous improvement of its processes to remain strong and competitive with its ever changing needs, demands and environment.

---

[4] *Business Process Benchmarking: Finding and Implementing Best Practices*, Camp, Robert C. ASQC Quality Press, 1995

Process improvement is necessary when processes are not meeting their expected measurements, when the competition is overwhelming your organization, when costs are getting out of hand, or when people's performance is dropping off. It is most often done in conjunction with process management. The major value add of process improvement is that it seeks not only to ensure the process is working as expected but also attempts to make the process even better.

Sometimes even more radical changes are needed to processes. This is process redesign, re-engineering, or innovation, which is defined as "The fundamental rethinking and radical redesign of business processes to achieve dramatic improvements in critical measures of performance (cost, quality, capital, service, speed)".[5] While riskier than continuous improvement, re-engineering may be necessary when an important process is performing very poorly and affecting the operation and success of an organization. It is a top-down strategic decision to bring about dramatic improvements and changes in the organization. True re-engineering is not just another word for layoff or downsizing. It is serious and very dramatic process improvement.

In summary, process improvement takes the results of benchmarking and the root causes of problems in the processes and attempts to develop alternative solutions or approaches. It reviews any potential solutions with process stakeholders and gains agreement for the best way to proceed. It pilots any improvements to see if they will really work; it measures the

---

[5] *Reengineering the Corporation,* Michael Hammer & James Champy, Harper Business, 1993

results of the pilot and gets stakeholder feedback before the new process is fully implemented.

Question Nine: "How will we work?" — Teamwork

Significant gains in productivity or quality can be accomplished by teams of people working together pooling their skills, talents, and knowledge. While single individuals have great impacts on organizations, they rarely have the knowledge or experience to understand all important aspects of the critical processes in which they are involved.

As Peter Scholtes notes in *The Team Handbook*, "Besides this pooling of skills and understanding, teams have another distinct advantage over solo efforts: the mutual support that arises between team members."[6] Managing processes to satisfy consumers and achieve organizational objectives is hard work. A single person's commitment and enthusiasm can weaken over time. There is a natural synergy that develops when people work together toward the same goals. Every organization should consider the great advantage of building strong teams to understand and answer these twelve questions.

---

[6] *The Team Handbook*, Peter Scholtes, Joiner, 1989

Question Ten: "How will we tell about our services?" — Marketing

The consumer makes the decision whether it wants to use the products or services of a nonprofit organization. How much the consumer knows or how he or she feels about the organization is due, in large part, to the organization's decision as to how much time, money, and effort it will spend on convincing consumers to use its products or services. Accordingly, nonprofit organizations should view marketing as a process by which decisions are made by consumers and by the organization.

The American Marketing Association defines marketing as "the performance of business to consumer or user."[7] Marketing would appear to begin with the production or development of products and services and to end when they reach the consumer. In reality it begins when the providing organization has the idea for the product or service and it ends when the consumer is fully satisfied with using it.

Thinking ahead to the work to be done in developing a strategic plan for the organization, the marketing plan must bring three things together:

1. The **Market** of consumers the organization is going after,
2. The **Strategic Plan**, and
3. How the **Organization** is organized

---

[7] *Marketing*, Robert Hisrich, Barrons, 1990

Figure 4 Marketing

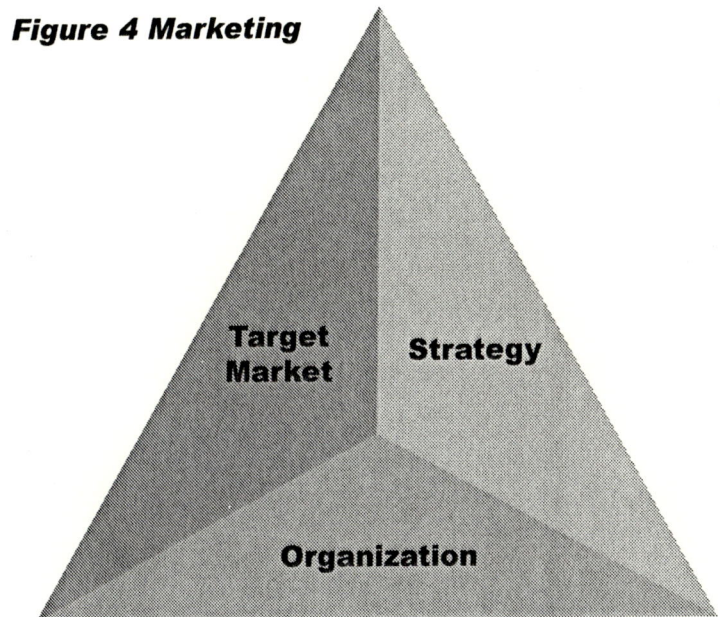

The target market after which the organization is going will have tremendous impact on its strategic plan. That market will be the locus of most of the organization's opportunities and many of its threats. It will be the focus of most of its objectives and action plans. And never forget that how you are organized or structured will affect the success of your strategic plan. The structure of your firm should follow your strategy.

Effective non-profit organizations integrate effective marketing into their overall operations.

The basic process is to:

1. Start with the original idea for offering a particular product or service to a set of consumers.
2. Take that idea and interview or survey potential consumers to see what they think about it.
3. Use their thoughts and suggestions to improve the starting idea.
4. Go back with the improved form and see what they think about it.
5. Once you have something that seems to meet your clients' or consumers' needs, define what it is being offered: what exactly is your offering?
6. An offering is any combination of products or services that satisfies the wants and need of a set of consumers within a particular market segment. (See page 59 for more information on market segmentation.)

With the offering defined, the organization should identify and forecast which and how many consumers will buy or accept it over time. Then it must marshal the capabilities of all its functions to meet consumer needs profitably and effectively.

There are five key aspects to marketing anything to clients or consumers:

- Demand Management
- Pre-Sales Qualification

- Closing the Deal
- Deployment or Delivery
- Support

Demand management involves two steps:

1. Identifying the demand for the offering; and
2. Managing the leads that identify specific segments or consumers that can be called upon to use your products or services.

You cannot provide a product or service if there is no demand for it (though too many organizations are so engaged). So the first step of marketing or getting your products and services accepted is determining how many consumers want them.

This can be done through market research, survey, word of mouth, asking about interest in your offering, or responding to consumer requests. When it is known how many potential consumers are interested in the offering, it is important to gather "leads" with the names of those potential users of your product or service. Marketing is easier when calling on people who have expressed a desire for the offering.

Pre-sales qualification involves ensuring that the consumers being called on really need the offering being provided and can carry out whatever terms and conditions are associated with receiving it. In a profit company this would be a credit check to make sure the consumer can pay for the offering or a qualification check to make sure they can properly and fully use it. In a non-profit situation, determining whether someone is qualified for the offering is usually fairly obvious.

Closing the deal is getting the consumer to agree to the contract or terms and conditions associated with he offering. It is certainly the most important step in marketing because it means the organization has succeeded in convincing the consumer to use its products and services. This step brings together all the talents and strategies the organization has devoted to the marketing effort.

Deployment or delivery is the actual providing of the product or service being offered. It may involve the packing and shipping of a specific product. It may be counseling a teenager. It may be building a house for a needy family. It may be healing a sick infant. And certainly it involves the completion of any paperwork or administrivia associated with the offering.

Support is ensuring that the product or service carries out its purpose and that consumers know how to use it properly. It is consumer care. Consumers may have questions about the service or want to express satisfaction or dissatisfaction with it. This step requires a phone number to call, a web-site to connect to, or a person to visit consumers using the offering.

The marketing process is not finished until consumers are satisfied with the offering. In words that resonate strongly within the nonprofit sector, Geoffrey Moore wrote in his *Crossing the Chasm*, "Fundamentally, marketing must refocus away from selling product and toward creating relationship. We must direct our attention toward creating and maintaining an ongoing consumer relationship, so that we can...see an abiding partner, willing to cooperate and adjust with us as we take on the day-to-day challenges. Marketing's first deliverable is that partnership."[8]

Question Eleven: "How will we lead our organization?"— Leadership

Leadership, and the credibility of that leadership, are among the bedrocks of any organization, and especially so in the case of nonprofit organizations so dependent upon their ability to develop and sustain interest and support from their diverse stakeholders.

Leadership is the first category assessed when organizations apply for the Malcolm Baldrige Award. In that case, leadership "examines how your organization's senior leaders address values, directions, and performance expectations, as well as a focus on consumers and other stakeholders, empowerment, innovation, and learning. Also examined is how your organization addresses its responsibilities to the public and supports its key communities."[9]

In *The Leadership Challenge*, James Kouzes and Barry Posner introduce and analyze five practices essential "to how to get extraordinary things done in organizations" (which is their book's subtitle. We have added the sixth practice for non-profit and for-profit organizations).

---

[8] *Crossing the Chasm*, Geoffrey Moore, Harper Business, 1991.

[9] "Criteria for Performance Excellence", Malcom Baldrige National Quality Program, National Institute of Standards and Technology, Washington, D.C., 2002

The six practices Kouzes and Posner and we posit are:[10]
1. Challenge the Process
2. Inspire a Shared Vision
3. Enable Others to Act
4. Model the Way
5. Encourage the Heart
6. Support the Public and Community.

The key commitments a leader must make to:

- To **Challenge the Process** are to:
  - search for opportunities
  - experiment and take risks
- To **Inspire a Shared Vision**, the leader must:
  - envision the future
  - enlist others into the vision
- To **Enable Others to Act**, the leader must:
  - foster collaboration
  - strengthen others to be able to act
- To **Model the Way**, the leader must:
  - set the example
  - plan small steps to promote progress
- To **Encourage the Heart**, the leader must:
  - recognize individual contributions
  - celebrate accomplishments

---

[10]*The Leadership Challenge*, James M. Kouzes and Barry F. Posner, Jossey-Bass, 1987.

- To **Support the Public and the Community**, the leader must:
    - recognize the impact of products and services on consumers and the community
    - be ethical and reach out.

Question Twelve: "Will our consumers be delighted? — Consumer Satisfaction

Consumers are looking for nonprofit organizations who know the answers to the ten questions just outlined. If your team thoughtfully explored and developed effective strategies to deal with these questions, then you are in a very strong position of having delighted consumers and having achieved your organization's purpose.

A nonprofit organization can improve itself by asking and answering these eleven questions with honesty and care. The answers will form the foundation for the organization's success in satisfying consumers and achieving the organization's objectives and purpose.

Chapter Two

Overview of the Strategic Planning Process

Question One: Where are we going? - Plan

To bring about consumer satisfaction and good organizational results, we need to develop a plan. Basically, that plan should address the following five questions:

1. Where are we now?
2. Where do we want to be?
3. How will we get there?
4. Who will do what, by when?
5. How are we doing along the way?

Addressing these basic questions leads the organization and its leaders to think strategically by providing a clear understanding of the particular character of all the elements of a situation.

For optimal effectiveness, the planning team gathered to address the organization's future should be comprised of individuals who represent all of the key areas of the organization to ensure all elements are considered. Their knowledge, orientation and experience will allow a more comprehensive overview of the nonprofit organization. By applying a tested and well-thought-out strategic planning methodology or process, as outlined in this book, the planning team and the organization exponentially increase their opportunity for success.

The Strategic Planning Process

Figure 5 provides an Overview of the Strategic Planning Process. This process contains six major steps.

Figure 5 Overview of the Strategic Planning Process

PURPOSE	1 External World	2 Internal World	3 Results Required	4 How	5 Implementation	6 Evaluation
Vision Mission	External Audit Market Analysis Assumptions Opportunities & Threats **Priority Issues**	Internal Audit *Process* *Quality* *Management* *Skills* *Structure* *Financial* Strengths & Weaknesses	Mission Statement Objectives	Strategic Alternatives ⬆ Strategies	Delegated Strategies Action Plans Project Process	Measures Review
GOALS	Where are we now?	Where are we now?	Where do we want to be?	How will we get there?	Who must do what by when?	How are we doing?

Step One (column 1)

Analyze the external factors over which you have no control. Things like:

- the economy
- your market
- your consumers
- sources for funding
- competition for services
- competition for funding
- sources and competition for volunteers
- government
- regulation
- socio-demographics
- technology
- potential partners
- factors of production

By carefully analyzing these or similar factors, you will identify the **Opportunities** and **Threats** facing your organization.

Step Two (column 2):

Consider the internal factors within your organization; things like:

- your processes
- your skills
- your resources
- your structure
- your management approaches
- your strategies
- your finances

By assessing these and other internal factors, you identify your **Strengths** and **Weaknesses**. (See page 41 for definitions).

Your Strengths, Weaknesses, Opportunities and Threats are known as your SWOTs.

From your SWOTs, you identify the key critical or Priority Issues (PI's) you must confront in developing your strategic plan. This is the first step in serious strategic thinking.

Five to seven Priority Issues will evolve from one or two particularly strong Threats, some serious Weaknesses, or a few very important Opportunities. The rest of the planning process is devoted to developing objectives and strategies to resolve these Priority Issues.

By virtue of completing steps one and two, these external and internal steps will answer the first question: **Where are we now?** This is also known as "situation analysis."

Step Three (column 3):

You now compare your key Priority Issues with your existing Mission Statement. This is the first step in answering the second planning question: **Where do we want to be?**

The mission statement should be related to the priority issues you identified in Step 2. If it is not, you should rewrite the mission statement, as it no longer reflects the most important issues facing your organization's goal to satisfy your consumers and your business needs.

Next you want to determine how to measure how your organization will meet the newly coordinated Mission Statement and Priority Issues. Specific, measurable and time-bound metrics must be created for each priority issue. These metrics will become the Objectives against which the eventual success of the strategic plan will be measured.

Step Four (column 4):

From the Priority Issues and Objectives, you identify **How will we get there?**

Start by identifying some potential Strategic Alternatives to achieve the Objectives. From three to five alternative strategies, the team will select the best one and create the final five to seven Strategies that will meet consumer and business needs identified in the priority issues.

Step Five (column 5):

With final Strategies developed, you answer the question: **Who must do what, by when?**

Delegate each of the Strategies to a sub-group of team members to develop a detailed set of Action Plans for making the strategy happen. The whole team will review, discuss, debate, and agree upon each set of action plans.

The larger team decides and allocates the time, people, and money resources needed for each Action Plan before each sub-group starts to implement its plans.

Step Six (column 6):

In the process' last stage you answer: **How are we doing along the way?**

You do this by deciding to come together every three to six months for the entire team to review and evaluate how each Action Plan is progressing in achieving its Strategy. These are dedicated sessions in which each strategy team briefly presents the status of what their group has accomplished, what they did not accomplish, the problems they need help with, any changes they recommend to their plans, how much of their budget they have spent, etc.

This periodic review session ensures that the nonprofit organization's plan stays dynamic and current because each team will apprise everyone about the real-world status of each Strategy. The entire team can make necessary changes to the plan at that time. It is a good idea to have review sessions once a quarter, but no less than twice a year.

Achieving Results

To develop the strategic plan requires a time commitment of three or four days from the nonprofit organization's top leadership – it's planning team. This time is necessary for both discussion and digestion of the myriad information necessary for setting your organization's future direction. This periodically updated plan will lay the foundation for everything the organization will do in the future.

In Chapter 3, we begin to outline the process you will follow to develop your strategic plan. In the context of our three to four day model, the overall process is:

First Half Day:

Part of the "THINK" stage, this is an introduction to the approach that will be taken over the next three days. In this half day, the methodology outlined in Figure 5, *Overview of the Strategic Planning Process* on page 33 is reviewed.

First Full Day:

Beginning the "AGREE" stage, the assembled planning group analyzes the external and internal factors and identifies the organization's Strengths, Weaknesses, Opportunities, and Threats. From these SWOTs, they determine the organization's strategic Priority Issues. The group selects market segments, identifies consumer wants and needs, discusses competitors, determines competitive advantage, lists its products and services, and reviews its financial position.

Second Full Day:

After reviewing or modifying the organization's Mission and Vision Statement, the team identifies how to measure Priority Issues and set strategic Objectives for each of them. They define potential strategic alternatives and choose the best to be the final Strategies for the plan.

At the end of the day, small teams will be assigned responsibility for each Strategy and will start developing Action Plans to implement them.

Last Day:

Reviewing and gaining consensus on the Action Plans for the Strategies, the assembled group allocates resources, determines a Review schedule, develops a financial forecast, and agrees on a final Mission Statement. They summarize the final plan and decide how to portray and communicate it to everyone.

Once a plan is in place, the strategy teams begin the "ACT" stage. Every 3 to 6 months thereafter, the Review process will be the "EVALUATE" stage.

In Chapter Three we turn to the specific work required to develop the nonprofit organization's strategic plan. A glossary of terms can be found in the Appendix on page 127.

Chapter Three

Gathering Information Prior to Priority Setting

The nonprofit organization's planning group begins its work immediately following its Introduction to Strategic Planning. Several days or weeks should pass before the full group reassembles to engage in collective priority setting.

During the interim period, all participants should work in one team or in small teams to analyze all external factors so as to identify Opportunities and Threats; and all internal factors so as to identify Strengths and Weaknesses. Combined, this gathering of information is called a SWOT Analysis.

- **Strengths** are the organization's current internal capabilities that are strong and will help meet key organizational needs.
- **Weaknesses** are current internal capabilities or lack thereof that prohibit the organization from meeting organizational needs.

- **Opportunities** are external trends, events, or ideas upon which the organization can capitalize to improve any aspect of its business situation.
- **Threats** are external trends, events, and situations—outside the organization's control—that must be planned for or mitigated.

In preparation for the priority-setting session (the first full day), the whole team or the smaller teams complete Tables 1 through 9, using the forms and worksheets provided in this book. These tables and forms are available on the website, as shown in the Appendix.

Worksheet 1:	Organization's External Factors
Table 1:	External Trends Summary Using Worksheet 1: The Organization's External Factors
Table 2:	Opportunities and Threats
Table 3:	Key Planning Assumptions
Table 4:	Key Market Segments
Worksheet 2:	Consumer Wants and Needs
Table 5:	Key Customer Wants and Needs Using Worksheet 2: Customer Wants and Needs
Table 6:	Key Competitors
Table 7:	Competitive Advantage

Table 8:   Products and Services

Table 9:   Finances

Separately, every individual on the planning team completes Tables 10 through 12:

Table 10:   Organization's Strengths, Weaknesses, Opportunities and Threats

Table 11:   Strategic Priority Issues

Table 12:   Focal Areas for Priority Issues

This collective and individual work provides the information the assembled planning group will use to develop your nonprofit organization's strategic plan.

The gathered information comes together on the first full day. At least the entire morning is taken up with presenting, discussing, and gaining consensus on Tables 1 through 9. Later, these tables will be a good source of information as the team develops its strategies. In the afternoon, the entire team uses Tables 10-12.

Based on the gathered information and everything it learns during this first full day, the group looks at its external and internal factors and reaches consensus on the organization's strengths, weaknesses, opportunities, and threats.

In addition to the worksheets and tables you use to gather the required information, we offer you examples of what the collected information might look like. These examples derive from our assumed Austin, Texas nonprofit, HelpingUHelp, which exists to serve the needy with food, clothing, adult and teen counseling, child services, skills training, and house repair.

Chapter Four

Environmental Assumptions

This section uses Worksheet 1 and Tables 1 through 3. Each of the following sections should be completed by the whole team or a small team.

Look at the External World and all those factors over which you have little or no control, but which will be very important to your success, to identify your nonprofit organization's Opportunities and Threats (column 1 of Figure 5, Overview of Strategic Planning Process).

Potential Environmental Factors

Start this analysis by identifying the external factors impacting the organization. Figure 6 provides an outline of potential external factors, including some unique ones for nonprofits.

Figure 6:
Potential Environmental Factors

Factor	Examples
Markets & Consumers	Growth or decline of markets Emergence of new segments New product/service categories Advertising / promotion method changes Changes in consumer needs and wants Price/cost trends New distribution methods
Competition	New competitors in market Changes in market share Changes in marketing methods, strategy Changes in financial conditions New products, services
Partners	Existing or potential partners to work with your organization
Economy	Interest rates Inflation / recession Consumer spending habits Foreign exchange rates Stock market condition

Figure 6:
Potential Environmental Factors, cont.

Government/Regulatory	City, State, Federal regulations Environmental issues OSHA / EPA regulations City, state, federal budget constraints
Sources for Fundraising	Potential contributors or donors Grants or Foundations
Competition for Fundraising	Organizations competing for funds
Market for Volunteers	All those places and organizations which can be considered for potential volunteers
Competition for Volunteers	Organizations competing for volunteers
Social/Demographic	Life style changes Population shifts Affluence levels Education levels
Technology	New equipment and systems Computer speeds and features Software availability New services available

Environmental Assumptions

Figure 6:
Potential Environmental Factors, cont.

Suppliers	Number of suppliers Power of suppliers Quality of suppliers Issues or problems with suppliers
Capital/ Equipment	Availability of funds/capital Availability of needed equipment
Materials / Utilities	Availability of needed materials Status of required utilities
Recruiting	Availability of new management skills Availability of skilled employee talent
Potential Entrants	Organizations that may be considering entering field Condition of industry for entry
Substitutes	Availability of substitutes for products to consumers
Complementors	Status of companies who may complement service or product
Others ???	Add any other factors that may apply to your organization

Based on a discussion and review of external factors impacting your nonprofit organization, use *Worksheet 1: The Organization's External Factors* to list those factors.

**Worksheet 1:
The Organization's External Factors**

1.
2.
3.
4.
5.
6.
7.
8.
9.
10.

**HelpingUHelp Worksheet 1:
The Organization's External Factors**

1. The Economy
2. Government / Regulatory
3. Recruiting
4. Market for Fund Raising
5. Competition for Funding
6. Market for Volunteers
7. Competition for Volunteers
8. Media
9. Public Perception
10. Relationships with Other Non-Profits
11. Technology

Having identified the key external factors, you now define the current trends or characteristics for each factor, deciding whether these trends will help or hurt your nonprofit organization in the future. Use Table 1: External Trends Summary for each external factor.

Helping trends will translate into Opportunities.

Hurting trends will translate into Threats.

In completing this trends analysis, use the model in Figure 7: Analyzing the External Environment.

For each factor, such as Funding Sources, identify its key trends. Look for real trends, not anecdotes or individual situations.

For each trend the team should determine whether the trend is important to the organization. When a trend is 4 or 5 in importance (high), ask how well the organization is handling or dealing with the trend. If the answer to handling is a 4 or 5, this trend is probably an Opportunity. If the answer is a 1, 2, or 3, the trend may be a Threat. Opportunities and Threats will be nouns and adjectives only.

Once the helping or hurting trends are identified, the team will want to review them in depth and define the specific Opportunities and Threats that result from those helping or hurting trends. Fill in Table 2 after the External Trends Summary form with the most important trends and the resulting Opportunities and Threats. These will be nouns and adjectives only.

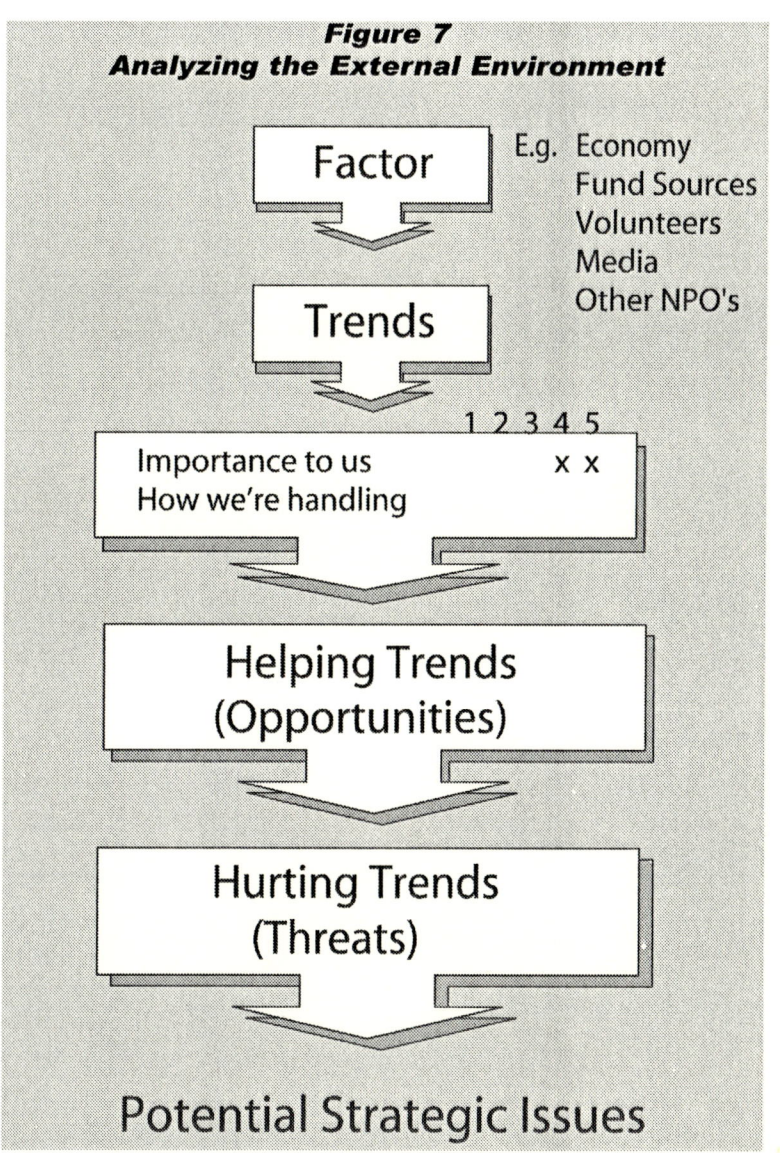

**Figure 7
Analyzing the External Environment**

Table 1: External Trends Summary

Factor:	
Helping Trends	**Hurting Trends**

HelpingUHelp Table 1: External Trends Summary

Factor: Economy	
Helping Trends	**Hurting Trends**
Low Inflation	Stock Market Drop
High Consumer Confidence	Indicators Down
Factor: Fund Raising Sources	
Helping Trends	**Hurting Trends**
Increasing # sources	Low Stock Market Impact
Positive Attitude	Bureaucracy
Factor: Fund Raising Competition	
Helping Trends	**Hurting Trends**
Our reputation	Increasing # of Nonprofits
Donor Loyalty	Competitive TV advertising
	Competitive Budgets
Factor: Market for Volunteers	
Helping Trends	**Hurting Trends**
Our Good Reputation	Attractive competitive terms & conditions
Good Client History	
Factor: Recruiting	
Helping Trends	**Hurting Trends**
Good Reputation	Poor Recruiting History
Our Facilities	High Wage Demands
Factor: Technology	
Helping Trends	**Hurting Trends**
Some IT Skills in Staff	Cost of Technology
	Complexity

Table 2: Opportunities and Threats

Key Helping Trends	Opportunities

Key Hurting Trends	Threats

HelpingUHelp Table 2: Opportunities and Threats

Key Helping Trends	Opportunities
Good Reputation	Greater Funding
Funding Sources	More Volunteers
Low Inflation	Better Community Support
Client History	New Partnerships
Consumer Confidence	More Efficient Operations
Positive Funder Attitude	More Locations
Little Regulation	Improved Staff Development
Volunteer Satisfaction	
Community Awareness	
Potential Partnerships	

Key Hurting Trends	Threats
Cost of Technology	Lower Funding
Technology Complexity	Lack of Volunteers
Poor Recruiting History	Less Grants
Staff Wage Demands	Poor Economy and Market
More Nonprofits	Technology Position
Competitive Advertising	Lack of Staff Recruits
Competitive Budgets	Competitors
Stock Market Down	
Volunteer Demands	
Changing Client Needs	

Environmental Assumptions

Planning Assumptions

Before continuing with external analysis, it is a good idea to define the basic assumptions upon which the plan is based and how to monitor their validity and change. Do this by reviewing the trends identified in Table 2 and selecting the most important to the organization and business.

Ask the question: underlying these trends are there any basic assumptions about the area of business or service we are in? For instance, is there a growing demand for services, or is government regulation predicted, or will sources of funds go up or down in the near term.

The trends or assumptions made should be ones that will significantly impact the organization and the strategic plan. Their validity must be monitored throughout the plan period and changes may necessitate revision of the plan.

In Table 3, list in column one the most important and critical assumptions concerning the future of the organization. In column two note the range within which results may vary without affecting the plan. In column three note the result expected if assumptions happen outside the tolerable range.

Table 3: Key Planning Assumptions

Assumption/ Key Trend	Tolerable Change	Result/ Response If Beyond Tolerable

HelpingUHelp Table 3: Key Planning Assumptions

Assumption/ Key Trend	Tolerable Change	Result/ Response If Beyond Tolerable
Inflation Stays Low	Up to 6%	New Economic Assumptions
Sufficient Funders	No less than 25	New Campaign Strategy
Sufficient Volunteers	No less than 100	Major Volunteer Recruitment
Sufficient Grants	At Least $100K	Board Grant Effort

Environmental Assumptions

Chapter Five

Market and Competitive Analysis

This section uses Worksheet 2 and Tables 4 through 8.

The objective of this module is to identify key market segments, key consumer sets, the most important consumer wants and needs, key competitors, competitive advantages, and products and services.

Segment Analysis

Your market is made up of a number of segments.

A segment might be differentiated by the type of service being used, by the manner in which the service is provided, by the type or size of a consumer, by the geographic placement of the consumer set, or some other demographic or behavioral characteristic.

To be successful, the organization should know what segments the organization is going after and as much about them as possible.

In column one of Table 4, list all potential segments the organization could serve, and in column two define the most important characteristics of each segment. These might be things like:

- largest segment
- critical social needs
- politically sensitive
- funding issues
- minority group

In reviewing possible segments to choose, you should decide the criteria to be used to select the segments to go after. In column three of Table 4 capture the criteria your organization will use to choose the segments to serve. Some criteria might be:

- profitability or revenue potential
- size of segment,
- consumer social need,
- consumer economic need,
- strategic fit with the organization's capabilities,
- cost or price sensitivity
- number of competitors,
- consumer affordability for the service,
- time needed to solve a problem,
- notable consumer behaviors in a segment,
- availability of substitute services.

Given the criteria, you should decide which of the listed segments satisfy them.

Identify the specific segments the organization wants to serve. Circle the selected segments in the first column of Table 4. Of potentially many segments in your marketplace, it is important that you carefully choose the ones you want to serve.

Table 4: Key Market Segments		
Segment	Characteristics	Criteria to Select

HelpingUHelp Table 4: Key Market Segments

Segment	Characteristics	Criteria to Select
Elderly	Transport Difficulty	Physical & Mental Capability
Youth	By Grade	Educational, Financial Need
Parents	Single, Multiple Married, Unmarried	Educational, Priority Needs
Hispanic	Spanish or Portuguese	Social Need
Afro-American	Largest Group	Social & Financial Need
Asian	Language	Social Need
White	Small group	Financial Need
Low Income	Poverty level test	Financial Need
Handicapped	Nature of disability	Physical & Financial Need

Consumer Wants and Needs

To identify the key wants and needs of consumers within the selected segments, list all consumer wants and needs the team can think of across all selected segments in Worksheet 2. Then identify the most important of these customer wants and needs in priority order in Table 5. Do this separately for each segment.

Worksheet 2: Consumer Wants and Needs

1.
2.
3.
4.
5.
6.
7.
8.
9.
10.

HelpingUHelp Worksheet 2: Consumer Wants and Needs

1. Personal and Caring Service
2. Variety of Services
3. Good Service Hours
4. Quality Service
5. Respect Client Values
6. Good Economic Results
7. Skill Building
8. Transportation Services
9. Education Opportunities
10. Technical Training

In Table 5, rank consumer needs in order of importance. List your organization's one to three top competitors in the segment and rank the organization and them on a 5-point scale on how each want and need is being provided for. For each want and need, note with an asterisk the ones your team is most interested in improving.

Market and Competitive Analysis

Table 5: Key Consumer Wants and Needs

Market Segment:

Major Competitors:
a.
b.
c.

Rating: 5 high - 1 low ***

Rank	Customer Want and Need	Us	a	b	c	Issue

HelpingUHelp Table 5: Key Consumer Wants and Needs

Market Segment:
Handicapped

Major Competitors:
a. DuPont NPO
b. Austin NPO
c. City Services NPO

Rating: 5 high - 1 low

Rank	Customer Want and Need	Us	a	b	c	Issue
1	Personal and Caring Service	3	5	4	5	***
2	Good Service Hours	5	5	2	3	
3	Respect Client Values	4	3	5	3	
4	Transportation Services	2	3	5	4	***

Importance vs. Performance

When the segments to be served have been identified, it is wise to interview or survey people who belong to each of the selected segments. Valuable information can be learned about what people really want and what they think about the providing organization.

Two questions should be asked to people in each segment:

- "What is important to you in seeking the services of our organization?" and
- "How well do you think our organization is doing in providing those services?"

With the answers to these questions, your nonprofit organization will really know what's important to your consumers and just how well you are doing in providing your services.

With these answers, it is good to build a simple two-by-two matrix such as this:

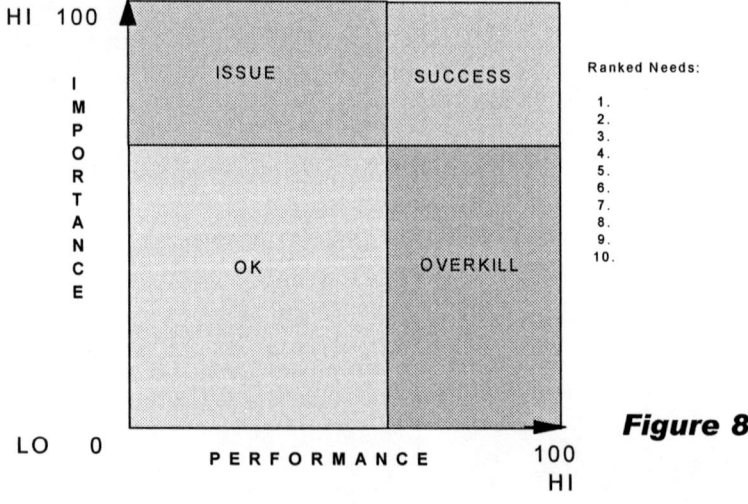

Figure 8

During the interview or survey, the consumer identifies some factor - say, caring service - and says it is 95 on the Y-axis scale of 100. The interviewer writes the factor to the right of the matrix as number 1 and marks a 95 on the Importance Y-axis. Then the consumer might say that your organization is doing a 40 job on the 100-point scale on the X-axis. The interviewer will now place a number 1 at the location on the matrix where 95 and 40 intersect. The interviewer will continue for every one of the five or ten factors that the consumer considers important enough to mention.

When the interview is finished, the final matrix might look something like this:

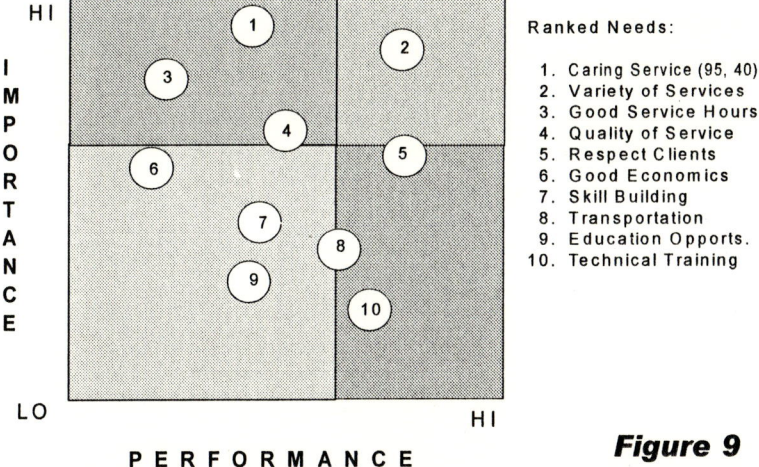

Figure 9

With this information directly from the lips of your consumers, your nonprofit organization knows exactly what its consumers want and need and what they think of the way your services are provided. This is a critical piece of information for any organization.

Market and Competitive Analysis

Clearly, factors that end up in the upper right hand corner are ones you are handling well. They are important to the consumer and you are performing well with them. Factors in the upper left spell trouble for you. They are important, but you are not performing well. Factors in the lower left are not important so you are not focusing on good performance. For factors in the lower right you are probably spending too much time or money to perform well for things not important to the consumer.

Competitive Analysis

Now it is time to identify in Table 6 those organizations that compete against your nonprofit organization or at least offer the same services to people in your market segments.

You need to understand their strengths and weaknesses, what services or products they offer, and your organization's major concerns about each of them. These will be used later in competitive or marketing strategies.

Table 6: Key Competitors

Competitor A	Strengths	Weaknesses
	Services	Concerns
Competitor B	Strengths	Weaknesses
	Services	Concerns
Competitor C	Strengths	Weaknesses
	Services	Concerns

HelpingUHelp Table 6: Key Competitors

	Strengths / Services	Weaknesses / Concerns
DuPont NPO	**Strengths** Personal Service Good Hours **Services** Counseling	**Weaknesses** Transport Client Values **Concerns** Personal Service Hours Open
Austin NPO	**Strengths** Values Focus Transport **Services** Transportation	**Weaknesses** Personal Service Poor Hours **Concerns** Transport
City Services	**Strengths** Personal Service Transport **Services** Training	**Weaknesses** Poor Values **Concerns** Training

Competitive Advantage

Competitive advantage is the answer to the question: "If consumers look at us in comparison to our top competitors, why will they choose us?" It is the way to beat the competition and win business or satisfy consumers in your selected segments.

Determine whether your organization has a competitive advantage in its area or business. This gives focus to all future work on programs that implement your organization's strategies.

A competitive advantage plays to:

Consumer needs	It must be based on highly ranked areas of consumer need
An organizational strength	Our capability to meet consumer needs is better than other organizations
A competitive weakness	The competition does not have this organization's capability to meet consumer needs.

To determine competitive advantages:

1. List your consumers' most important wants and needs from each of the Table 5's.
2. List the most critical of these in section one of Table 7;

Market and Competitive Analysis

3. In section two identify the capabilities needed or in place to address those needs. Capabilities may show up later as Strengths. Some examples are:

Need	Capability
Low price	Cost reduction
Large variety	Additional product selections
On-time delivery	Trucks and computer system
Good consumer service	Attitude and skills
Support services	Consumer help desk
Quality	Quality processes throughout

4. In section three, identify any competitive advantages that your organization currently has.

5. In section four determine what fixes or improvements in capabilities must be made to gain new competitive advantage. Things to be fixed may show up later as Weaknesses.

6. In section five write the new competitive advantages to be gained after improvements.

Table 7: Competitive Advantage

Top Ranked Consumer Needs (from Table 5)	Capabilities Required to Meet Needs
Current Competitive Advantage	
Areas to be fixed for Competitive Advantage	
Potential New Competitive Advantage	

Market and Competitive Analysis

HelpingUHelp Table 7: Competitive Advantage

Top Ranked Consumer Needs (from Table 5)	Capabilities Required to Meet Needs
Personal and Caring Service	Sensitive, trained staff
Good Service Hours	Larger budget for hours
Good Economic Results	Business Skills and contacts
Skill Building	Better training processes
Transportation Services	Buses and drivers
Current Competitive Advantage	
Awareness of county services	
City Council contacts	
Good Education Staff	
Areas to be fixed for Competitive Advantage	
Improved Training Processes	Better Recruiting
More Volunteers	Bigger Facilities
Better Measurements	Better Planning
Potential New Competitive Advantage	
Training Focal Point	
Efficiency of Operations	
Best Volunteer Team	

Products and Services

It is now important to identify the products and services your organization provides to consumers. These provide Opportunities and come from Strengths. Given current products and services, look also for new products and services and new segments. In so doing, you identify new Opportunities.

In the first column of Table 8, list current products and services. In column two, show the criteria used to select them. These will signify why the products or services were chosen and give ideas for new products or new uses. In column three, rate the products relative to how well they are currently performing with consumers. Some Weaknesses may be discovered for later use.

On the second page of Table 8, get creative and think of some new products or services that might work in existing segments. Then consider better ways to penetrate or succeed in those segments. Determine whether there are other, new segments that could be approached for existing products and services. Consider whether some of these new products might appeal to new segments.

At the end of the second page, identify all the product and service opportunities to add to the Opportunity list.

Table 8a: Products and Services (A-C)		
A. **Current Products & Services**	**B.** **Criteria for Selecting**	**C.** **Average Rating (5 high - 1 low)**

HelpingUHelp Table 8a: Products and Services (A-C)

A. Current Products & Services	B. Criteria for Selecting	C. Average Rating (5 high - 1 low)
Counseling	Social Need	4
Skills Training	Job Opportunities	3
House Repair	Living Needs	2
Child Services	Number of Children	3
Teen Counseling	Teen Problems	4
Food	Need	5
Clothing	Need	5

Table 8b: Products and Services (D-H)

D. New Products/ Services in existing segments

E. Ways to penetrate existing markets

F. New segments for existing Products/Services

G. New Products/Services in new segments

H. New Opportunities Identified

HelpingUHelp Table 8b: Products and Services (D-H)

D. New Products/ Services in existing segments
Drug Counseling
Psychological Counseling

E. Ways to penetrate existing markets
Client Surveys
Open House

F. New segments for existing Products/Services
University personnel
Bus and train passengers

G. New Products/Services in new segments
Financial Services
Mapping Services

H. New Opportunities Identified
Drug & Psychological Counseling
Financial Services
Mapping Services

Financial Analysis

Knowing how your nonprofit organization is performing financially is essential to your success. While finances are part of the Internal Analysis, they are considered here since they are so impacted by external factors.

Table 9 provides a useful tool in this regard:

1. List the most important financial measures in your organization in column 1: the ones you use to keep track of any and all of your financial matters. Add to or replace the samples provided.

2. Show your organization's past three-year history for these measures in column two.

3. Show this year's budget in column 3.

4. Show your forecast for the next three years in column 4.

5. Your column 4 forecast will be revised and continually updated by your planning team and financial officer as your new plan is put in place and evolves.

Table 9: Finances

Measures	History 3 Fiscal Year			Budget This Fiscal year	Baseline Forecast Next 3 Fiscal Years		
	1999	2000	2001	2002	2003	2004	2005
Total Market Size							
Revenues							
Revenue Growth Rate							
Salaries							
Operating Expenses							
Capital Expenses							
Volunteer Expenses							
Special Events							

HelpingUHelp Table 9: Finances

Measures	History 3 Fiscal Year			Budget This Fiscal year	Baseline Forecast Next 3 Fiscal Years		
	1999	2000	2001	2002	2003	2004	2005
Total Market Size	70	85	98	110	115	122	130
Revenues	100	130	145	160	175	190	220
Revenue Growth Rate	10%	12%	15%	18%	19%	20%	22%
Salaries	800K	845K	900K	950K	1.15M	1.25M	1.33M
Operating Expenses	200K	235K	267K	300K	298K	318K	335K
Capital Expenses	185K	200K	242K	274K	300K	328K	340K
Volunteer Expenses	95K	104K	120K	130K	140K	150K	160K
Special Events	40K	48K	52K	55K	62K	73K	85K

Chapter Six

SWOTs and Priority Issues

Working individually, rather than as the planning team, you should complete Tables 10 to 12 by eliciting the opinions of those who work for and with you, as well as your board members. Ask them what they think are your organization's Strengths, Weaknesses, Opportunities and Threats (SWOTs). Then conclude what your opinion is on these and write it in the tables.

Table 10 is Strengths, Weaknesses, Opportunities, and Threats (SWOT).

Earlier, your planning team analyzed the external factors to identify Opportunities and Threats. Now, you, as an individual team member, will look at internal and external factors and identify Strengths and Weaknesses, Opportunities, and Threats.

Figure 10 shows a good model for finding the trends that will translate into Strengths and Weaknesses.

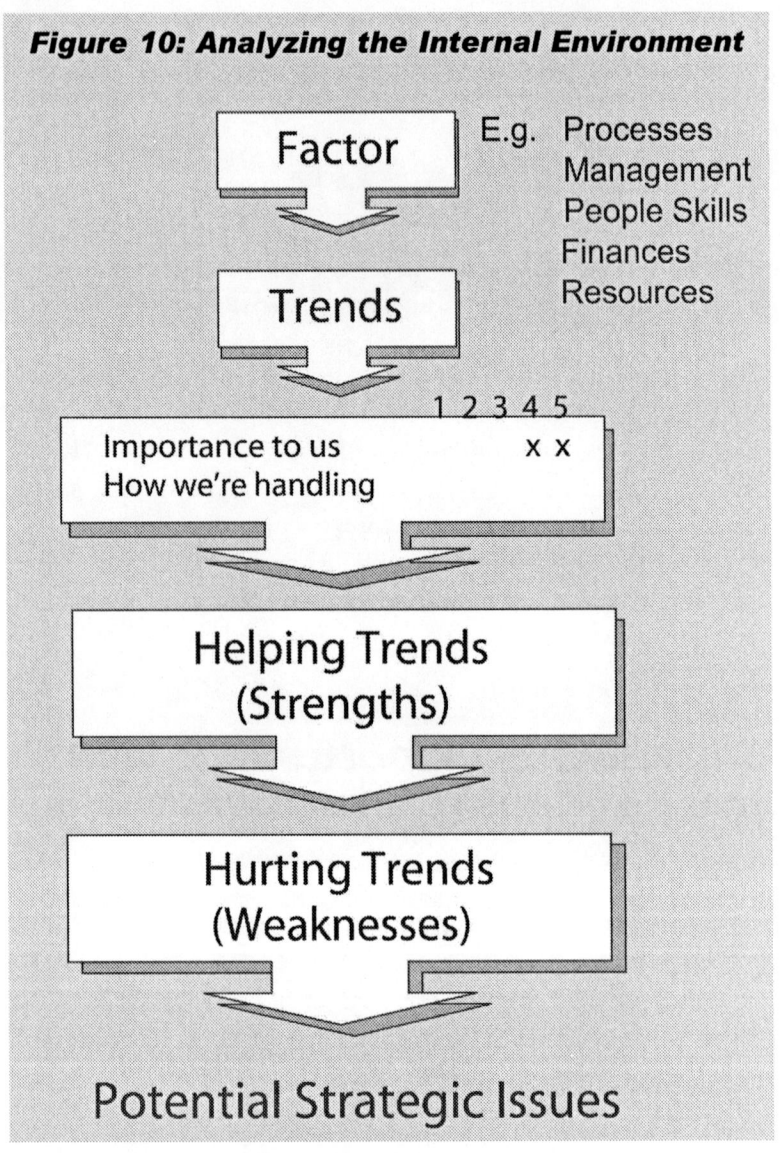

Figure 10: Analyzing the Internal Environment

To determine the internal factors, consider, for example, the organization's processes, management approaches, people skills, finances, structure, resources, and current strategies. From these, it is possible to see what your organization is good and not so good at doing.

In the first morning session, your team may have come up with different Opportunities and Threats from the ones each individual will identify here. That doesn't matter. In the afternoon, you will choose the most relevant from the two sessions.

As an individual, identify ten to fifteen of each SWOT, then prioritize them and list no more than the top five of each. These will be nouns and adjectives only.

Table 10: Organization's Strengths, Weaknesses, Opportunities, and Threats (SWOTS)

Strengths	Weaknesses
Opportunities	**Threats**

HelpingUHelp Table 10: Organization's Strengths, Weaknesses, Opportunities, and Threats (SWOTS)

Strengths	Weaknesses
Reputation	Poor Internal communications
Dedicated Staff	Poor Recruiting
Flexibility	No Strategic Plan
Good Volunteers	Few Measurements
Training Skills	Limited Facility Space

Opportunities	Threats
Greater Funding	Poor Economy
New Partnerships	Competitive Services
More Efficient Operations	Decreased Funding Sources
Improved Staff Development	Volunteer Disinterest

Table 11 is Strategic Priority Issues (PIs).

Looking at all the SWOTs in your Table 10, decide what the critical issues facing your organization are and write them in Table 11. These critical issues become the strategic Priority Issues from which you and your nonprofit organization will develop your objectives, strategies, and action plans in the planning process.

A Priority Issue may arise:

- From an Opportunity or two that a specific strength can win
- From a serious Threat or two;
- From a Weakness or two to be fixed.

Be creative in turning SWOTs into Priority Issues.

Table 11: Strategic Priority Issues

HelpingUHelp Table 11: Strategic Priority Issues
Restructure and improve the FUNDRAISING process
Encourage and build new PARTNERSHIPS within the nonprofit community
Improve all internal and external COMMUNICATIONS
Improve ability to RECRUIT and retain good staff
Create systematic, effective STAFF DEVELOPMENT, orientation, and training
Develop set of MEASUREMENT tools and processes to enhance performance

A Priority Issue (PI) is action-oriented and should be shown in sentence form with a verb.

Table 12 is Focal Areas for Priority Issues.

Decide what key focal areas must be defined to resolve the Priority Issues. What are the things to measure for success? Write each priority issue in the first column of Table 12 and the focal area to be measured in the second column.

If the Priority Issue is "We need to raise more money", then some Focal Areas (FA) are:

Total Funds Raised,
Number of Donors, and
Grants Provided

With the Focal Area (FA), indicate how it should be measured in the third column. E.g., using our fundraising example:

Dollars for Total Funds Raised,
Number for Number of Donors, and
Number and Dollars for Grants

These ideas for Focal Areas will be used on Day 2 during the development of Objectives.

Table 12: Focal Areas for Priority Issues		
Priority Issue	**Focal Areas**	**Measures**

HelpingUHelp Table 12: Focal Areas for Priority Issues

Priority Issue	Focal Areas	Measures
Fund Raising	Funds Raised Donors in Place Grants Provided	Dollars Number Number/ $$$
Partnerships	New Partnerships Type of Organization	Number Organization Type
Communication	Communication Methods Audience	Type of Communication Communicators
Recruiting	Potential Recruits Actual Recruits Recruiting Staff	Number Number/ % Number/ Job
Staff Development	Staff size Development Areas Staff Trained	Number Topical Area Number/ Skill

Consensus on SWOTs and Priority Issues

At this point, in the afternoon of the first day, the facilitator will gather everyone's Strengths one at a time and list them on a flip chart. After listing 15 or 20 of them, eliminate similar words and agree, as a planning team, which are the five to seven most important Strengths for your nonprofit organization. Thereupon, the facilitator will write these final Strengths on a different chart.

A similar process is followed for Weaknesses, Opportunities and Threats.

As Opportunities and Threats are listed, the planning group compares them to the ones you identified at your earlier group session.

At the end of this part of your strategic planning process, the facilitator posts the final list of five to seven SWOTs so all can review them. Thereupon, your entire planning team decides the organization's Priority Issues, by:

- Looking at Threats to see if any are so serious they must become a Priority Issue;
- Looking at Weaknesses to see if any are so serious they must become a Priority Issue;
- Looking at Opportunities to see if they are important enough to be a Priority Issue.

In doing this, the group's members may review their Table 11 for ideas on final Priority Issues (PIs).

The final Priority Issues that will become the foundation for the creation of your nonprofit organization's Strategic Plan derive from the list of ten to twenty PIs from the above process, which the planning group will reduce to the five to seven most critical.

With the Priority Issues defined, the facilitator will ask attendees to share the Focal Areas they defined in Table 12. These will lay the foundation for determining the Objectives to be set for each Priority Issue in the next day's session.

Your facilitator posts the final PI's for all to see and concludes your first full day by summarizing all you have agreed upon, as contained in the day's charts. Following this session a summary of the charts is distributed to all planning team members to serve as the basis for the Objective and Strategy Setting component of your nonprofit organization's strategic planning process.

Chapter Seven

Objective and Strategy Setting

The Strategic Planning process is now entering its second full day. All the analysis and preparation to date have brought you to the point where your nonprofit organization can thoughtfully set its objectives and strategies to achieve organizational success.

A reminder: organizational success is defined as meeting the requirements of your consumers and achieving the purposes and objectives of your organization.

Mission Statement Review

With your Priority Issues in hand, it is time to compare them to your organization's Mission Statement. This is column 3 of the Strategic Planning Process Overview chart on page 33.

Recognizing that the Priority Issues have been determined by your planning team as part of the current process, and that your Mission Statement may have been written years ago, it is critical to review the Mission Statement in light of current Priority

Issues. These PI's will more accurately reflect your present organizational and consumer needs than the old Mission Statement.

If there is a difference in perspective between these key organizational tools, you ought to consider rewriting or modifying the Mission Statement to be more current and focused on today's needs.

Any rewrite of the Mission should be assigned to a person or small team. They should be charged with bringing a draft of the revision to the next planning group meeting. Any final revisions should be completed in time to be in consonance with and included within the final plan.

Focal Areas and Measures

With key Priority Issues identified, all participants have a good idea of the areas around which to build the strategic plan. With that in mind, develop some measures to use later in determining whether those issues were resolved.

At the first planning group meeting all participants identified the things they would want to measure for the PI's in Table 12. Start with those Focal Areas and agree as a team what the Measures for each of them should be.

The Priority Issues and Focal Areas can now be aligned with the proposed time frame of the strategic plan. To do so, the planning team should decide the number of years for which they are developing the strategic plan.

The plan should be for at least one year and perhaps as many as three to five years.

If it is to be a 3-year plan, then the facilitator should start a new flip chart with five columns for each Priority Issue:

			Objective		
PI	FA	Measure	2004 (next year)	2005	2006

Each participant should suggest a Focal Area (FA) relating to the Priority Issue (PI) and the facilitator should write it on a new chart. In recommending a Focal Area, the team member should also tell how it will be measured.

There is no limit to the number of FA's for a PI. However, each one should be agreed upon by the entire team. A focal area will be a measurable element of a priority issue.

Objectives

This process continues until each Priority Issue has a number of Focal Areas and Measures connected with it.

A SMARTS objective should be established for each Focal Area, reflecting the quantity or number the planning team wants to set as an Objective for each of the three years. This may be a certain dollar amount, a quantity, or a number to be achieved in the future.

These Objectives will become the ways to measure the accomplishment of the PI's and the Strategies into which they will develop.

SMARTS objectives are:

Specific   in that it focuses on certain Focal Areas (FA)

Measurable   in that a numeric or quantitative goal has been defined

Assignable   in that one of the team members will be responsible for it

Realistic   in that it is doable

Time bound   in that there is a date by which it should be accomplished

Stretching   in that the team sets improving numbers each year.

An example of Objective development is:

			Objective		
PI	FA	Measure	2004	2005	2006
Restructure	Funds Raised	Dollars	$800K	$1M	$1.2M
Fundraising	Donors	Number	25	30	40
	Grants	Dollars	$100K	$120K	$150K

Strategic Alternatives

With your nonprofit organization's Objectives now in place, review the Priority Issues to focus on what the goals are.

Review the tables from Day 1 to recall information on segments, consumer wants and needs, competitors, competitive advantage, and products and services.

At this point everyone on your planning team should let their minds roam freely and allow the facilitator to capture everyone's creative alternatives for dealing with the Priority Issues. This is shown in column 4 of the Strategic Planning Process Overview chart on page 33.

While the ideas expressed at this point may not be the final solutions to be chosen, they could open minds to new ways of thinking and acting. These are the potential strategic alternatives to consider in developing final strategies.

With suggestions from the planning team, the facilitator should list these ideas on Table 13 in the order of the pain that they might create in and for the organization.

From this list, choose the alternative that best seems to resolve the specific Priority Issue.

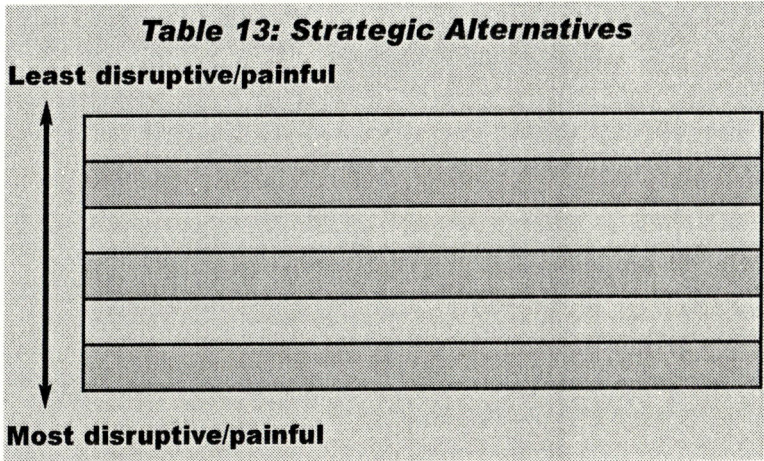

Table 13: Strategic Alternatives

Least disruptive/painful

Most disruptive/painful

Objective and Strategy Setting

As an example, assume the priority issue is "Raise more funds for future needs." These might be some strategic alternatives:

HelpingUHelp Table 13: Strategic Alternatives

Least disruptive/painful

Send letter to all donors for new fundraising
Hire external communications specialist
Hire Development director
Improve our donor contribution campaign to raise more money
Develop new management methods for fundraising
Change priorities and policies for partnerships in fundraising

Most disruptive/painful

Final Strategies and Strategy Teams

To create the final Strategies, start with the preferred strategic alternative and add some numbers or quantitative goals from your Objectives. This will result in a more powerful strategy statement.

For instance, assume one Priority Issue is *Raise more funds for future needs*, and the potential strategic alternative is *Improve our donor contribution campaign to raise more money*. If one Objective is to *Raise an additional $1,000,000 by 2005*, then your Strategy might be *Use an improved donor campaign to raise $1,000,000 for future needs by 2005.*

Once Strategy statements have been developed for all of the Priority Issues, the planning team must study them carefully and decide which will be the final Strategies.

Review each Strategy one by one and determine the skills required to implement it. Given the various skills of all team members, assign a team leader and a team of two to three to be responsible for each Strategy.

As a team, they will develop programs made up of various action plans.

Action Plans

Each strategy team should meet to develop a detailed Action Plan for each Strategy. This is column 5 of the Strategic Planning Process chart on page 33.

Using the Action Plan Form A, identify the Strategy, the team leader, the team members, and the most important long-term and short-term goals for the Strategy.

Long-term goals are for the length of the plan—one to five years.

Short-term goals are for the first 25-33% of the plan.

Next the planning team should decide every activity or action that must be achieved to successfully implement the Strategy. These will not be high-level, philosophical or theoretical actions, but will be every specific thing that must be done to make the Strategy work. Most teams will come up with ten to thirty or more actions.

As each activity is identified in Action Plan Form A as **"What"**, the team assigns it to a person and lists that person's name under **"Who"**. Finally, the date by which the activity or action must be accomplished is shown on the form under **"When"**.

When all actions are defined, the team determines how many of those actions will require assistance or involvement from another department, function, or process not under the control of their department or group. Identify those groups on the attached Action Plan Form A1 and show what is required of each of them by when.

Some examples of coordination required may be: your function's approval from Finance for spending; training of your process team by Human Resources; or Marketing's input on pricing a product.

In most cases, Action Plans will evolve into or impact key *processes* or *projects*.

Process is a related area from the second question at the beginning of this document. As we said,

"Processes are the vehicles through which real work gets done in any organization. They are, in essence, what organizations do to achieve their purpose."

Many projects may evolve from the Action Plans.

The plan developed here will not succeed if the organization does not coordinate and focus on the processes and projects involved in implementing its Strategies and Action Plans.

Action Plan Form A

Strategy:

Team Leader:

Team:

Long-term goals	Short-term goals

Step	What	Who	When
1			
2			
3			
4			
5			
6			
7			
8			
9			
10			

HelpingUHelp Action Plan Form A

Strategy: Fundraising

Team Leader:
John Smith
Team:
Mary Jones
Jim Johnson
Alice Cooper

Long-term goals	Short-term goals
$1.2 million by 2006	$800 thousand by 2004
50 Donors in Database	30 Donors

Step	What	Who	When
1	Hire Development Director	John	Nov 2002
2	Develop 2003 Budget	Mary	Nov 2002
3	Determine program expenses	Alice	Dec 2002
4	Submit budget to Board	John	Dec 2002
5	Review Fund Raising with Board	John	Dec 2002
6	Set up special events calendar	John	Jan 2003
7	Develop Donor Package	Jim	Jan 2003
8	Develop Print Advertising Plan	Jim	Feb 2003
9	Revitalize Church Relations	Alice	Mar 2003
10	Hold Church special event	Alice	Jun 2003

Action Plan Form A1

Coordination Requirements for Strategy:

Group/ Dept./ Person	What's Required	When

HelpingUHelp Action Plan Form A1

Coordination Requirements for Strategy: Fundraising

Group/ Dept./ Person	What's Required	When
Executive Director	Approve hiring of Development Director	Oct 2002
Director of Finance	Approve Fund Raising Budget	Nov 2002
Board of Directors	List of Potential Donors	Jan 2003

Review

All the parts of a strategic plan are now in place.

The teams assigned to each Strategy will begin implementing their Action Plans in the near future.

As they do this, they will have some success, some failure, and some frustration. They may begin to realize that some of the assumptions, opportunities, threats, strengths, or weaknesses are not as the team defined them during the planning process. They may find the segments were not as expected, the competition was not as weak as estimated, or the consumers did not have the wants and needs the team had expected.

In other words, the plan will not seem to be as good as the team had hoped.

There is an important and simple solution to keep the plan dynamic and current. It is shown in column 6 of the Strategic Planning Process Overview chart on page 33.

Every three months (six at the most), your entire planning team should come together for a Review session as shown on Form B.

Measurements from the Objectives developed in Column three will be tracked and reported in this Review. By the end of the planning session, the team should set the date for the first Review session.

All future Review sessions should be relatively short meetings:

1. Each team presents using a format similar to Form C.

2. Each team shares what they have accomplished in their Action Plans, what they did not accomplish and why, what problems they had, what plans, resources, or timing they would like adjusted.

3. Each team reports on how well they are meeting the measurements set in their Objectives and indicates whether the Objectives should be changed.

4. After all teams have presented their concise and brief presentations, in approximately 15 minutes the other team members spend another fifteen minutes commenting on and discussing all points. They then reach a consensus on changes, adjustments, or concerns.

5. Each Strategy team should then summarize the conclusion and indicate what their Action Plan will be until the next Review session.

Review - Form B	
Purpose	**Method**
Anticipate issues	Periodic evaluation
Fix Problems	Responsible executive and team
Redirect focus, resources, plan	Key results
Motivate key people	Objectives achieved, not achieved
Measure people and results	Problems, issues
	Key metrics

Quarterly Review- Form C

___ Quarter, 20___

Strategy:

Team Leader:

Long-term goals	Short-term goals

Bring your original objectives and action plan sheets to the Review session

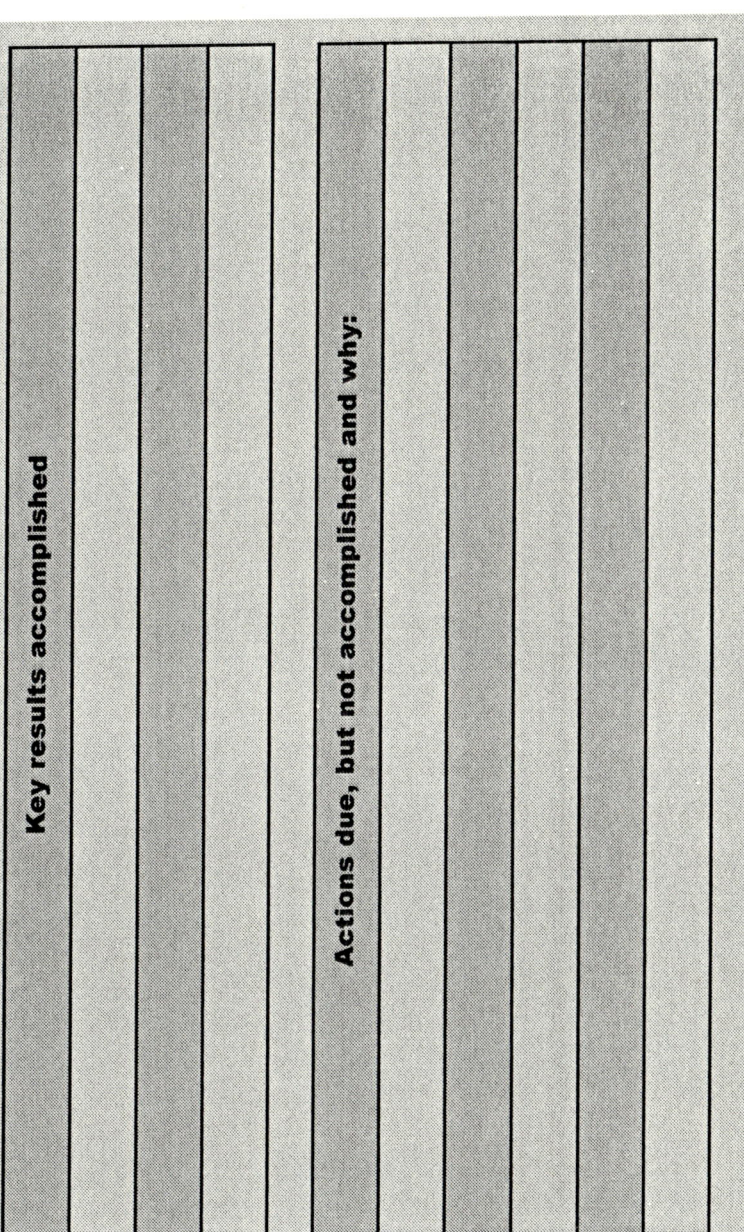

Quarterly Review- Form C, cont.

Strategy:

Problems/ Issues to be addressed and when

Changes in timing, objectives, resources requested:

Status of Objectives set for Strategy or Program

Spending vs. Plan

Actual	
Planned	
Difference	

Other Comments:

HelpingUHelp Quarterly Review- From C

1st Quarter, 2003

Strategy: Fundraising

Team Leader:
John Smith

Long-term goals	Short-term goals
$2 million by 2005	$1 million by 2003
50 Donors in Database	30 Donors

*****Bring your original objectives and action plan sheets*****

Key results accomplished
2003 Budget in Place and Approved by Board
Hired Development Director

Actions due, but not accomplished and why:
Donor Package not complete. Board gave too few potential donors
Press Advertising not complete. Newspaper strike in January

HelpingUHelp Quarterly Review- Form C, cont.

Strategy: Fundraising

Problems/ Issues to be addressed and when
Donor package to be completed by March
Press Advertising Plan to be completed by April

Changes in timing, objectives, resources requested:
Church Relations Special Event to be delayed until September at request of five major churches

Status of Objectives set for Strategy or Program

Have commitments for $850,000 in donations

Have identified 23 donors to date

Spending vs. Plan

Actual	$105,000
Planned	$120,000
Difference	$15,000

Other Comments:
Need more support and involvement from the Board

Plan Wrap Up

Once all Action Plans are in place, your planning team reviews and allocates resources to the teams. It may be necessary to adjust some Action Plans in their people, timing, or financial resources. It is easier and more effective to adjust resources at this point than to have the Strategy teams decide that resources do or do not exist as they are developing their Action Plans.

To do resource allocation, the team must ask if the organization has the people, time, and funds to achieve each Strategy.

It is a good idea to start by allocating available funds to sustaining and improving the existing organizational purpose and programs. Then allocate other available funds to newly defined strategic programs based on:

- Alignment with Mission
- Long-term financial impact
- Timeframe of program
- Resource availability
- Infrastructure requirements
- Legal requirements
- Risk

If there are conflicts or inadequate funds, consider:

- Shifting timing of a Strategy or program
- Cutting back on some aspects of the Strategy
- Reducing resources on other programs
- Outsourcing or using temporary resources
- Identifying other sources of funds or resources

At this point, it is important to allocate people, time, and financial resources to the various Action Plans. With that done, the team should be led by the Financial Director or coordinator to review the baseline forecast from Table 9 and develop a new financial forecast for the entire planning period.

Use the same financial measures from that table and forecast them for the next one, three, or five years.

If it was decided on day 1 to rewrite or modify your current Mission Statement, that work should be agreed upon and completed at this point,

With all elements of the plan decided, the team now decides the final form for presenting it to your nonprofit organization's stakeholders.

The plan should be brief, clear, and concise. A recommended format is shown in Form D.

The main body of the final plan document should show the Mission and Vision of the organization, the Strategies chosen, their measurable Objectives, and their detailed Actions Plans. End this section with a description of the periodic Review process.

Other important information should be shown as an Appendix. Key historical and recent financial data is appropriate. A summary of the details the team determined in the early stages of the process can be useful and of interest to readers of the plan. These are such things as the Assumptions, Strengths, Weaknesses, Opportunities, and Threats. Show here the original strategic Priority Issues from which the team developed the final Strategies.

The last thing the team should do is to decide how they will communicate the final plan to your board, all your employees, and all other stakeholders.

Outline of a Strategic Plan - Form D

A. Mission / Vision

B. Strategies

C. Objectives

D. Action Plans

E. Review Process

Appendices

A. Financial Records
   1. Current Financial Statement
   2. 3-5 Year History
   3. 3-5 Year Forecast
   4. Cash Flow Analysis History/Forecast

B. Strategic Summary
   1. Assumptions
   2. Strengths
   3. Weaknesses
   4. Opportunities
   5. Threats
   6. Priority Issues

Ideally, every participant in the planning process made it a point to interview employees, board members, and other stakeholders to get their opinions about SWOTs, segments, competitors, and other topics of the various sessions. In that case, the final plan will not be a surprise to them at the end.

Conclusion

All twelve questions have been understood and answered. We have spent a good deal of time sharing ideas for answering the first of these and developing a powerful plan for achieving your organizational goals. We showed you how answering the last eleven questions will help your team think more strategically in bringing together that plan. They are the actions you must take and the tools you must use to make that plan happen.

It is hoped that this framework will encourage and guide your people to work together to focus on the needs of your consumer and bring continued success to your organization.

Glossary

Action Plan

A set of steps that will be undertaken to implement the programs to achieve a strategy. It defines who will do what by when. It should show the program objectives to be achieved, the resources required, and the targets it plans to reach. *It is through these that the strategic plan gets implemented.*

Core competencies

Those unique internal capabilities, technologies, and skills that provide a sustainable competitive edge through a company's product or service line. *These are your organization's greatest strengths.*

Focal Areas

The important areas that you will want to measure in setting specific objectives to achieve your priority issues or strategies.

Measures

The specific and usually quantitative criteria that you will use to evaluate the success of meeting your strategic objectives for each focal area.

Mission Statement

Defines the purpose of your business, its consumers, its direction, its future thrust, and its internal and external values.

Objective

The specific, measurable, assignable, realistic, timebound, and stretching targets you set for each focal area. *These are the key things by which you will measure the success of your plan.*

Opportunities

External trends, events, situations, and ideas that you can capitalize on to increase future profits, revenues, consumer satisfaction, market share, and/or your competitive advantage. *These include emerging market segments, new products and services, geographical expansion, new technology, a weak competitor, cost reduction, and better communications for increasing market penetration.*

Planning Assumptions

Key assumptions your company is making about important factors affecting your business, such as segment potential, economic situation, government regulations, consumer desires and habits, competitive situation, quality and availability of suppliers, employment, costs and prices, etc.

Programs

Coordinated actions that will be used to implement a strategy and accomplish strategic objectives. *This is where the strategy becomes operational and hands and feet replace the brain.*

Review

That ongoing series of meetings to be held by the planning team after the strategic plan is in place to evaluate the status of each action plan in achieving the strategies, to anticipate issues, to fix problems, to redirect resources, and to motivate and measure people and results. *Ideally, review sessions should be held approximately quarterly.*

Strategy

Specific areas of action that will result in the achievement of your strategic objectives, your strategic thrusts, and your priority issues. These are the main drivers of your plan.

Strengths

Current internal capacities that are strong and will help you meet key consumer needs, and, ideally, are superior to those of the competition. *These sustain your competitive advantage in the marketplace.*

Threats

Possible external trends, events, and situations—outside your control—that you must plan for or plan to mitigate. *These include competitors, their actions, onerous legislation or regulation, declining markets, consumer dissatisfaction, and bad trends in any environmental factors.*

Vision Statement

A succinct statement of what your organization wants to accomplish and where it hopes to be in the future.

Weaknesses

Areas in your current internal capabilities that prohibit you from meeting consumer needs or achieving a competitive advantage. *These need to be fixed quickly to avoid losing consumers, profits, or market share.*

Appendix

Strategic Planning Forms on the Internet

The strategic planning forms found in this book are available on the web at:

http://1stworldlibrary.com/Michael_Dore/tablesforms.htm

You many download and photocopy them for use in your organization provided that you do not remove or obscure all or any part of the copyright information.

About the Author

Michael S. Doré specializes in strategic planning and management, process improvement, quality management, and marketing. He holds an MBA in Management from the University of Maryland.

Mr. Doré is president of MSD Resources and a Principal in Planning Resources Associates. He was formerly a senior consultant with the IBM Consulting Group and was manager of quality for the $3 billion, 17-country IBM Latin America business unit. He also held other key domestic and international management positions at IBM in marketing, finance, planning, and business practices.

Mr. Doré has consulted with clients in the pharmaceutical, oil, health, banking, financial, manufacturing, computer, energy, investment, nuclear, protein, beverage, and not-for-profit industries. He has worked extensively with non-profits in the Austin, Texas area, developing business and strategic plans. He has led seminars and managed projects or training for more than 2000 executives and professionals in strategic planning, process management, quality management, marketing, and transformational leadership. He has consulted and taught for four years for the American Management Association nationwide and globally.

He teaches Strategic Management, Quality, and Operations Management in the St. Edward's University MBA and New

College programs in Austin, Texas. He teaches courses in Strategic Planning and Quality for the National Graduate School. He presents monthly for Austin Community College's Center for Community-Based and Nonprofit Organizations, and leads seminars for the University of Texas Professional Development Center.

He has managed a market-driven business process re-engineering project at the American Bible Society and has taught business process re-engineering to a major division at Coca-Cola. He developed and taught courses to a major Wall Street bank in strategic planning, process management, quality management, and marketing. He led major go-to-market efforts for IBM Latin America as a consultant, and facilitated hundreds of customer workshops for the Texas Utilities Corporation (TXU).

Contact Information:

Michael S. Doré
President
MSD Resources
rmdore@att.net

About the Collaborating Editor

Barry Silverberg, 1st World Library's Managing Editor for Nonprofit Leadership, Management and Organizational Development series, served as senior editor for this volume. Mr. Silverberg is founding Director of the Center for Community-Based & Nonprofit Organizations at Austin Community College. His 30 years of diverse volunteer and professional leadership within the nonprofit sector includes service as Chief Professional Officer of Jewish Federations in Syracuse, NY and Austin, TX, president of the Texas Association of Nonprofit Organizations (TANO), founder and president of the Syracuse Area Interreligious Council and leadership roles in many other nonprofits.

About the Publisher

1st World Library is in the business of making dreams come true. We enable authors just like you to easily and rapidly transform their works into printed books available for sale to the public. 1st World Library is a self-publishing company.

If you are writing to share stories, personal experiences, the lessons you have learned along the way, we will help you create a book that will be cherished and shared by others.

If you are writing to facilitate the learning of others, the skills and knowledge that you have gained, we will help you create a book that will become a standard.

If you are writing for posterity, from a sense of responsibility to those that follow, we will help you create a book that your children's children will cherish.

Through our combined experience, the contributions of our partners, and the technology that is available today, we provide you with the best tools and experience available to self-publish. As an author, you will be supported, encouraged and guided along the way.

Authors interested in exploring self-publishing opportunities through 1st World Library should contact: info@1stworldlibrary.com. Please provide us with a short synopsis of your book (maximum of one page) and your contact information, including the best time for us to call.

Authors' Note: We have found an initial discussion of our services and what you can expect from us is very helpful in making your decision. During this initial discussion we will explain the self-publishing process clearly; you will then understand your responsibilities and just how much you can expect to spend.

Brad Fregger
Founder/President/CEO
1st World Library - The World's Publisher
brad@1stworldlibrary.com
(512) 339-4000
www.1stworldlibrary.com

Index

A

act, 5-7, 28, 39
action plan, 19, 23, 33, 36-37, 39, 89, 103-124, 127-128
adaptablity, 14, 17
Afro-American, 63
agree, 5-7, 26, 36, 38, 94, 98
alternatives, 7, 20, 36, 38, 100-102
Asian, 63
assignable, 100, 128
assumptions, 33, 42, 45, 56-57, 112, 123-124, 128
Austin Community College, 134-135

B

Balanced Scorecard, 15-17
Baldrige, Malcom, 18, 27
baseline, 83-84, 123
Bean, L.L., 18
benchmarking, 3, 13-14, 17-20
benefit, 4, 14
budget, 37, 47, 53, 55, 76, 82-84, 109, 111, 119
Business Process Benchmarking, 18-19
Business Process Re-Engineering, 18-19

C

Camp, Robert, 18-19
campaign, 4-5, 57, 102-103
capabilities, 24, 41, 60, 63, 73-76, 127, 129
capital, 20, 48, 83-84
challenge, 1-2, 5, 9, 26-28
closing deal, 25-26
communications, 14, 89-90, 93, 102, 128
community, 28-29, 55, 90
competitive advantage, 18, 38, 42, 59, 73-76, 100, 128-129
competitive analysis, 59, 70-72
Community-Based and Nonprofit Organizations, 134-135
competitors, 38, 42, 46, 55, 59-60, 65-67, 71-73, 100, 125, 128-129
complementors, 48
concerns, 70-72, 113
Customer Driven Company, The, 11
consumers, 1-4, 10-18, 21-22, 24-27, 29, 31, 34-36, 38, 42, 46, 48, 53, 55, 59-60, 64-65, 68-70, 73-77, 97-98, 100, 112, 125, 127-129
context, 9, 11, 13, 15, 17, 19, 21, 23, 25, 27, 29, 38
core competencies, 127
criteria, 27, 60-63, 77-79, 127
Criteria for Performance Excellence, 27
Crossing the Chasm, 26-27

D

D-Day, 4
delighted, 3, 29

delivery, 25-26, 74
demands, 19, 24-25, 53, 55-56
demographic, 34, 47, 59
departmental, 4, 104
deployment, 4-5, 25-26

E

economy, 34, 46, 49, 51, 53, 55, 89
effectiveness, 9, 13, 17, 23-24, 29, 32, 90, 122
efficiency, 13, 17, 76
elderly, 63
enable, 28, 137
encourage, 28, 90, 125, 137
entrants, 48
environmental factors, 45-48
equipment, 10, 47-48
evaluate, 5-7, 14, 17, 33, 37, 39, 113, 127-128
expense, 83-84, 109
external, 10, 18, 33-35, 38, 41-43, 45-53, 56, 82, 85, 90, 102, 127-129

F

factor, 2, 6, 34-35, 38, 41-43, 45-50, 52-53, 69-70, 82, 85, 87, 128-129
financial, i, 2, 38-39, 46, 63, 81-82, 122-124, 133
focal area, 43, 91-93, 95, 98-100, 127-128
for-profit, i-1, 18-19, 27
forecast, 24, 39, 82-84, 123-124

functional, 4
fundraising, 47, 90-91, 102, 108, 111, 118, 120

G

glossary, 39, 127-129
government, 18, 34, 47, 49, 56, 128
growth, 46, 83-84

H

handicapped, 63, 67
helping, 50-55, 86
Hisrich, Robert, 22
hispanic, 63
history, 53, 55, 82-84, 124
hurting, 50-55, 86

I

importance, 4, 50-51, 65, 68-69
innovation, 16, 20, 27
In Search of Excellence, 5
infant, 26
inspire, 28
internal, 10, 16, 18, 33-35, 38, 41, 43, 82, 85-87, 89-90, 127, 129

J

"Just do it", 5

K

Kaplan, Robert, 17
Kouzes, James, 27-28

L

leaders, 1-2, 4-5, 27-29, 32, 103, 106, 108, 114, 118
leadership, i, 3, 27-28, 37, 133, 135
Leadership Challenge, The, 27-28
low income, 63

M

market, 22-25, 33-34, 38, 42, 46-47, 49, 53, 55, 59, 62-63, 66-67, 70, 80-81, 83-84, 128-129
marketing, 3, 22-27, 46, 70, 104, 133-134
material, 10, 48
measurable, 10, 36, 99-100, 123, 128
measurement, 3, 15-16, 20, 33, 76, 89-90, 112-113
measures, 11, 15, 17-18, 20, 33, 36, 38, 82-84, 91-93, 98-100, 113, 123, 127-129
military, 4
minority, 60
mission, 7, 33, 35-36, 38-39, 97-98, 122-124, 127
model, 28, 38, 50, 85
Moore, Geoffrey, 26-27

Index

N

National Institute of Standards and Technology, 27

Norton, David, 17

O

objective, 7, 12-13, 15, 21, 23, 29, 33, 35-36, 38, 59, 89, 91, 95, 97, 99-102, 112-114, 116-118, 120-121, 123-125, 127-129

opportunity, 1-2, 4-5, 7, 23, 28, 32, 34-35, 38, 41-43, 45, 50-51, 54-55, 65, 77, 79-81, 85, 87-90, 94, 112, 123-124, 128, 137

organization, ii, 1-5, 9-27, 29, 32, 34-39, 41-43, 45-50, 56, 60-61, 65, 68-70, 73-74, 77, 82, 85, 87-89, 93-95, 97, 100-101, 104-105, 122-123, 125, 127, 129, 131, 134-135

overview, 31-33, 35, 37-39, 45, 97, 101, 112

P

parents, 63

partner, i, 26, 34, 46, 137

partnership, 27, 55, 89-90, 93, 102

payback, 1-2

perception, 49

performance, 11, 13-14, 17-20, 22, 27, 68-70, 90

Peters, Tom, 5

philosophy, 5, 15

plan, 2-6, 9-11, 14-15, 19, 22-23, 28-29, 31, 33, 36-39, 43, 56, 82, 89, 95, 98-99, 103-106, 108-114, 117-118, 120-125, 127-129, 133

Posner, Barry, 27-28

priorities, ii, 14, 33, 35-36, 38, 41, 43, 63-64, 85, 87, 89-95, 97-103, 123-124, 127, 129

process improvement, 3, 19-20, 133

process management, 3, 13-14, 18, 20, 133-134

process redesign, 20

process re-engineering, 20, 134

product, 1, 12-13, 15, 18, 22, 24-26, 29, 38, 43, 46, 48, 59, 70, 74, 77-81, 100, 104, 127-128

public, i, 18, 27-29, 49, 137

purpose, 1-6, 10, 26, 29, 33, 97, 104, 113, 122, 127

Q

qualification, 6, 24-25

quality, 3, 12-15, 18-21, 27, 33, 48, 65, 74, 128, 133-134

R

re-engineering, 20, 134

realistic, 100, 128

recruiting, 48-49, 53, 55, 57, 76, 89-90, 93

regulatory, 47, 49

relationship, 26, 49

result, 1-2, 7, 13, 19-21, 31, 33, 37, 50, 56-57, 65, 76, 102, 113, 115, 119, 129

revenue, 60, 83-84, 128

S

salaries, 83-84

satisfaction, 2-3, 11, 14-15, 18, 26, 29, 31, 55, 128

Scholtes, Peter, 21

segments, 24-25, 38, 42, 46, 59-68, 70, 73, 77, 80-81, 100, 112, 125, 128

service, i, 1, 3, 12-13, 15, 18, 20, 22, 24-26, 29, 34, 38, 43-44, 46-48, 56, 59-60, 65, 67-72, 74, 76-81, 89, 100, 127-128, 135, 138

skill, 21, 33, 34, 44, 48, 53, 65, 74, 76, 79, 87, 89, 93, 103, 127, 137

social, 47, 60, 63, 79

source, 34, 43, 47, 50, 53, 55-56, 89, 122

specific, 5, 15, 25-26, 36, 39, 50, 61, 90, 100-101, 104, 127-129

stakeholder, i-ii, 1-2, 11, 13, 20-21, 27, 123-125

statements, 4, 33, 35-36, 38-39, 97-98, 102-103, 123-124, 127, 129

strategic plan, 2, 4, 5, 10, 22-23, 33, 35, 36-39, 43, 56, 89, 95, 98, 112, 124, 127-128, 133

strategically, i-ii, 1, 9, 32, 125

strategy, 4, 7, 15, 23, 26, 29, 33-39, 43, 46, 57, 70, 73, 87, 89, 95, 97, 99, 101-106, 108, 110-114, 116-118, 120-125, 127-129

strengths, 4-5, 7, 33, 35, 38, 41, 43, 70-74, 77, 85-86, 88-90, 94, 112, 123-124, 127, 129

stretching, 100, 128

substitute, 48, 60

suppliers, 48, 128

support, 21, 25-29, 55, 74, 121

SWOTs, 35, 38, 41, 85, 87-91, 93-95, 125

T

target market, 23
Team Handbook, The, 21
teamwork, 3, 21
technology, 27, 34, 47, 49, 53, 55, 127-128, 137
teenagers, 26
thinking, i-ii, 1, 5-7, 9, 22, 35, 101
threats, 4, 7, 23, 33-35, 38, 41-43, 45, 50-51, 54-55, 85, 87-90, 94, 112, 123-124, 129
time bound, 36, 100, 128
trends, 42, 46, 50, 51-57, 85-86, 128-129
twelve questions, 3, 9, 11, 21, 125

U

utilities, 48, 134

V

value, 10, 12, 15, 17, 20, 27, 65, 67, 72, 127
vision, 11, 14, 16, 28, 33, 38, 123-124, 129

W

Waterman, Bob, 5
weaknesses, 4-5, 7, 33, 35, 38, 41, 43, 70-74, 77, 85-86, 88-90, 94, 112, 123-124, 129
white, 63
Whiteley, Richard, 11

X

Xerox, 18

Y

youth, 63

Printed in the United States
15555LVS00001B/256-279